Praise for *A Southern Psychic's Guide to Fixin' the BIG BUT Syndrome*®

"Fixin' the Big BUT is the Big Breakthrough we have been waiting for. This book contains everything you need to live the life of your dreams. By following the guidance provided by Soul Intuitive Eddie Conner, you can have everything in life you ever wanted; from a loving relationship with your mate to improving your relationship with money and career, and your creator."

– Victor Benoun
– Author of *Your Castle, No Hassle*

"After reading Eddie's unique and funny perspective on how we all can self-sabotage ourselves with our BIG BUTS, I am ready to look my BIG BUT in the mirror and make some changes. With humorous stories, insightful observations and great depth, Eddie coaches and cheer-leads us all to a place where we have choices and freedom to be, do, and have what we want in life– NO BUTS about it!"

– Karen Drucker
– Inspirational Recording Artist

"Eddie Conner can kick my BIG BUT anytime! Being a writer myself, I truly appreciate the simplicity of using BUT armor "Punctuation Shields" like the period to stop a contradicted

desire in its path–it's so simple. Now try using "and" to link your first desire with another pure focused intention! Eddie's techniques empower you to feel good, appreciate all you have, and kick BUT big time. Thank you for your light and energy."

– Arlene Zimmerly
– Author of *Gregg College Keyboarding & Document Processing and Keyboarding Connections*

"Eddie, Thank You for helping us all realize that life doesn't have to be about our BIG BUTS!"

– Taaffe C. O'Connell
– Actress/Publisher/Named Who's Who in the World

"Don't let the humor, warmth, and down-home flavor of Eddie Conner's Fixin' the Big But Syndrome fool you; he shares some seriously important, and liberating wisdom. Never before has so much light been wonderfully shined on one of the biggest thought-nullifiers in our vocabulary. Well done!"

– Adam Abraham
– Publisher/Author of *I Am My Body, NOT!*

"By following Eddie's advice in this lively, funny book, I was able to kick my own BUT problem and begin living a richer, fuller, BUT-free life!"

– Brian A. Wilson
– Hollywood Writer/Director

"This book shows you how to get your beliefs and your desires on the same energy level. From this new perspective, you will be able to soar your way to success."

– John Livesay
– Author of *The 7 Most Powerful Selling Secrets*

"Eddie Conner has written an exuberant, enlightening book on the "yeah buts" that muddle up our thinking and stop us from our good. When your BIG BUT gets you down, pick up this entertaining treasure filled with wonderful tools to lighten your load."

– Chellie Campbell
– Author of *The Wealthy Spirit*

"Author Eddie Conner empowers his readers to get off their ass and Fix the BIG BUT Syndrome by leaving their BUTS behind and making their dreams come true with simple tools and loving humor."

- Jacquie Jordan, TV Producer / Media Consultant
- Author of, *Heartfelt Marketing,* and *Get On TV!*

"A Southern Psychic's Guide to Fixin' the Big BUT Syndrome is a lot of fun to read. Plus, it gives readers more than a few easy and practical ways to obliterate our BIG BUTS!"

- Jami Gibson
- Author of *Psychic Journal with Coloring Meditations*

Other Books by Eddie Conner

How to Get Your Travel Freq On!

Meditation CDs

Dolphin & Whale Communion
A Temple of Angels
Angels, Dolphins, and Whales

Presentation CDs

5 Ways to Create an Amazing Life
Think It, Feel It, Manifest It
Get Your Money Freq On
Money and the Soul Conscious Mind
Magnetizing Money
OMG! How Did I Attract This?
The BUT Secret and The LOW of Attraction

Presentation DVDs

Living the Hi-Frequency Life

A Southern Psychic's Guide to Fixin' the BIG BUT Syndrome®

Eddie Conner

Published by Eddie Conner / Soul Awareness

Second Edition; First Printing

Eddie Conner – All Rights Reserved®
The Big BUT Syndrome – All Rights Reserved®

Soul Awareness / Eddie Conner
3940 Laurel Canyon Blvd. #138
Studio City, California   91604

EddieConner.com

Cover Design by Jeff Dannels

All rights reserved. No part of this book may be reproduced or transmitted in any form or by any means, including but not limited to information storage and retrieval systems, electronic, mechanical, photocopy, audio recording, video recording, or syndication, etc., without the written permission from the copyright holder.

ISBN 978-0-9972600-2-1

I dedicate this book to Momma and Soapy.
You both have always been my first and
greatest source of inspiration.
I love you.

Contents

The Backstory: A Southern Psychic in Los Angeles….......xiii

Foreword……………………………………………..........……xvii

Preface…………………………………………………..……...xix

A Note to the Reader………………………………....…....xxv

Introduction…………………………………………..………1

Section One: The Problem

CHAPTER 1	Defining the BIG BUT Syndrome®……9
CHAPTER 2	Proceed with Caution: BUT Zones Ahead……………………………..23
CHAPTER 3	Symptoms of the BIG BUT Syndrome …………………….…....…29
CHAPTER 4	The OVAL Mirror® of Life…..…….....…33
CHAPTER 5	The 1-2-3's of Your B-U-T……………41
CHAPTER 6	The Truth about Yeah, BUTS…..………47
CHAPTER 7	The Infamous Invisi-BUTS…..………..49
CHAPTER 8	BIG BUT Understudies and Stand-ins on the Stage of Life…...……53
CHAPTER 9	Riding the AND Avalanche…….….....63
CHAPTER 10	Super Hero Punctuation Shields – BUT Armor…………….……………...75

Section Two: The **SOUL***ution*

CHAPTER 11 Ten BUT BLASTERS –

Soul Tools to Fix Your BIG BUT…..81

BUT BLASTER ONE: The TAGS Technique……...85

BUT BLASTER TWO: Feeling Good……………......88

BUT BLASTER THREE: Laughter and Humor……….91

BUT BLASTER FOUR: Nature……………….…….94

BUT BLASTER FIVE: Music and Harmonics….…..101

BUT BLASTER SIX: Praying with a Pure Heart...106

BUT BLASTER SEVEN: Vibratory Vocabulary…….109

BUT BLASTER EIGHT: Artistic Expression……......112

BUT BLASTER NINE: Visualization and

Imagination……………….119

BUT BLASTER TEN: Daydreams and

Night Dreams……………..123

CHAPTER 12 The BUT Blaster Workout………...129

CHAPTER 13 The Feel Good Life………………133

CHAPTER 14 Your Soul Affirming Oath……....…135

A Sincere Thank You………………………………139

About the Author…………………………………..141

Memoirs of a Southern Psychic -

Ghosts, Angels, and Other Deep-Fried Miracles...143

Acknowledgements

I want to thank my amazing friend Victor for encouraging me to transform a two-page class outline into this book. I am grateful to my dream team: Jami, Mike, Ramona, Rose, Brian, Jeff, Cynthia C, Cynthia R, Barbara, and Robert for your love, creativity, and professional guidance.

Special thanks still to Chellie, John, Karen, Taaffe, Jacquie, Arlene, Mary Ann, Maureen, Adam, James, Mary, Evelyn, Tim, Debbie, Ellen, David A, Kathy, Allison, DJ, David T, Karen N, Karen M, Janice, Melissa, Jill, Marissa, Jeff M, Nick, RJ, and to all my friends, clients, and associates! I could not have accomplished a project of this magnitude without your continued love and support. No Buts About!

* * * * * *

I want send a special note of appreciation to my most influential spiritual teacher, Abraham-Hicks Publications, for being pure, passionate teachers. Your wisdom is loving, healing, and life-changing. I attribute my ability to complete this project directly to your priceless message that we all have the power to change our physical circumstances with our invisible attributes. Thank you for the light you generously share with millions.

The Backstory: A Southern Psychic in Los Angeles

In the spring of 2004, I wrote and published this book under the title, *Kicking the Big BUT Syndrome®*. I was thrilled with its success, original content, and cheeky cover. Twelve years later I've decided to change the cover and refresh the title.

Since its initial release, people still ask me why I wrote it. My answer. I believe in this material and know firsthand this subject matter creates fantastic results, if you use it.

I first realized the Big BUT Syndrome was an epidemic as a result of doing Soul Intuitive readings for 25 years. Since 1990, I've noticed contradictions in my client's energy when they talked about their love, money, and career. It turns out that it's a very rare person that can speak their desires without contradicting them.

Aristotle said it best, "Don't doublespeak." Meaning, don't talk about what you do want and what you don't want in the same sentence.

When we doublespeak, our desires are canceled out by our negative beliefs. When we speak about our desire for money, and follow that desire with a negative belief that we don't have enough money, we, in that exact moment have contradicted our monetary desires. And guess where that puts us? Right back where we started from. Stuck. In the rut. Of the Big BUT Syndrome.

I'm happy to repackage this material because it has made me, and others aware of our habitual contradictions, something I call, BUT-tradictions. Truth be told, there are Love-Buts, Career-Buts, Money-Buts, Body-Buts, and a heck-of-a-lot-more BIG BUTS roaming the planet, each waiting to block or stop your heart felt desires.

Instead of combing the Universe for every single BIG BUT out there, *A Southern Psychic's Guide to Fixin' the BIG BUT Syndrome®* focuses on your love, money, and career.

I've been obsessed with metaphysics, spirituality, and the law of attraction since I was old enough to run barefooted and gnaw on a good hunk of fatback. Because I am a Soul Intuitive, which is a persnickety word for psychic, I also love the paranormal, the subconscious mind, and our human energy fields. I have pulled from each of these categories and wrapped everything I've learned about BIG BUTS into a cozy blanket of humor and lightheartedness.

Why this approach? Because I have been to seminars, Sunday School services, and studied self-help books that are dry, clinical, and way too serious for my attention span. The heavier the material felt to me, the harder it was for me to retain it. If I couldn't retain it, I wasn't inspired to use it. For me, the better I feel about something, the more likely I am to remember it, apply it, and get results from it.

So guess what? *A Southern Psychic's Guide to Fixin' the BIG BUT Syndrome®* is deliberately light, animated, and simple, because simple is powerful.

One last thing. I was fresh off the turnip truck when I arrived to Los Angeles in 1995. I was wet behind the ears and naïve to the sheer magnitude of the radio opportunity gifted to me while being a guest psychic on STAR 98.7. Because I was born and raised in the foothills of North Carolina, my southern accent was so strong that Angelinos would politely ask me to repeat myself, hoping to understand my country bumpkin twang.

What I once thought of as my linguistic defect among the beautiful people walking red carpets turned out to be a huge blessing in disguise. My downhome drawl had organically made me stand out among my peers. Which led to more amazing radio, magazine, and television opportunities where journalist, hosts, and deejay's called me affectionate nicknames like, "Another Guy from Mayberry," and "John Boy Walton's Love Child."

Twenty-one years after landing in the City of Angels, I still have a southern drawl that pushes the boundaries of single syllable words. I still eat collard greens, cheese grits, biscuits, and fat-back with gravy, and I'm warmly referred to as, A Southern Psychic in L.A., which is why this book is titled, *A Southern Psychic's Guide to Fixin' the BIG BUT Syndrome®*

On that note, let's have fun learning about how you may be sabotaging your desires, and I'll share principles that can lift you up and out of your poverty thinking, and firmly put you back into the driver's seat of prosperity consciousness.

Sounds like a plan right? I think so too. Settle back. Relax. Allow me to share a few innovative ways that you can put your BIG BUT behind you and improve your love, money, and career.

Foreword

It is so fitting that this book is written by Eddie Conner. I have known Eddie for a decade, and he never disappoints me in his ability to choose to feel good and make all those around him feel good too. Eddie is a magnet for powerfully positive thoughts and feelings. You just cannot be around him and not be laughing and playing and having a great time. But Eddie is serious about feeling good. There is a science behind his claims, and there are powerful "manifestors", like myself, who have used Eddie's techniques and attracted exactly what they wanted for their lives.

Someone so happy must have been born into the perfect circumstances, right? Not Eddie. In fact, he was born in a less-than-ideal situation and he was truly grateful for every blessing that came his way. Through his innate intuition, humor, and desire to make his mama happy, Eddie learned to recognize the positive side of everything. Science would later support his idea that we are living in a hologram that is a reflection of our expectations and intentions. The more sweet, positive, and loving thoughts and feelings we send out, the more we receive.

If your world is a hostile, unforgiving, and apathetic place, ask yourself, "Where am I feeling hostile?" and send forth compassion; "Who do I need to forgive?" and let the slight go; and, "What don't I care about?" and learn something about that thing. When you bring joy to others, you will feel joy. You cannot avoid it. Conversely, when you contradict your dreams and goals with a BIG BUT, you cancel any way the Creator of the Creation has of delivering up your order.

Eddie makes this lesson a fabulously fun course of study. Remember when Mary Poppins sang, "A spoonful of sugar makes the medicine go down"? The BIG BUT Syndrome is a sweet way of helping us accept a bitter truth, i.e., that we sabotage ourselves. And through wisdom, exercises, and suggestions, it provides the remedy. You can heal this syndrome, and the medicine is in this book. You are holding the miracle cure for your life. Get ready to laugh and love and grow rich.

Cynthia Richmond

Author of *The Dream Power Journal,* and

Dream Power: Use Your Night Dreams to Change Your Life

Preface

When I called Momma and told her I was working on a new book, she was thrilled. Then I told her the material was about, "Kicking the Big BUT Syndrome."

There was a deafening silence on the other end of the phone.

"Momma?" I said.

Chirping crickets seemed to fill the 2,600 miles between my place in Los Angeles and my momma's home in High Point, North Carolina.

"Momma, it's a cool idea. It'll help a lot of people."

There are times when you don't really want peace and quiet. This was one of those times! At last, Momma cleared her throat. "Edward," she began, pausing for dramatic effect as mothers often do.

My imagination took off as if someone had fired a start's pistol. My mind raced, across the country and back through time, until I was a child again, growing up in "the Projects" of North Carolina. Looking back, it seems like a tough place to start. But at the time, it was all I knew, and Momma made it home for me and my brothers.

When I was five, we "moved on up" to a mobile home. A single-wide, if you must know! Yep, – I lived in a trailer park. Again, not the nicest living conditions perhaps, but it gave me the greatest of luxuries: time. I had a lot of time to sit and think and just…be. It was during this time that I started to realize that I heard things, saw things that my wacky brothers and overbearing father and step father did not see. My psychic abilities were making themselves known to me.

Daydreaming and tapping into my psychic impressions helped me escape the crushing poverty and violence of my childhood.

As I moved into high school, I started to realize my gifts could help others answer questions and solve problems related to their own lives. That made them feel good, and I also realized that it made me feel good, and gave me purpose.

I had a string of "regular" jobs – fry cook at The Sizzler, Calendar Machine Operator (please, don't ask!) in the textile mill – but none of them gave me the satisfaction I was after. It was time to seek out something more.

With some urging from my best friend, Tim, I packed my bags, said my good-byes, kissed my Momma and moved to Los Angeles.

I came to Dreamland to pursue my dreams. During my eight years here in the city of angels, I've tapped deeper into my psychic abilities, enhance my "soul awareness" and have helped hundreds of people reshaped their lives. Living my dreams was helping other people live theirs!

The more people I helped, the more I noticed a pattern in their lives. The biggest problem people have is not any lack of ability or lack of desire or any other lack; it seems to me their biggest problem is getting in their own way. And what gets in our way the most? Our big BUTS: the BUTS that stop us, the BUTS that slow us down, the BUTS that make us hesitate, and especially the BUTS that cause us to contradict our desires with negative emotion.

I want to get rid of every "BUT" in America. Heck, every "BUT" in the world! And this book is my way of doing exactly that, one BUT at a time…starting with your "BUT!"

Everything I've come to understand, every good and bad and humbling and exhilarating experience I've had since I was an eight-year-old boy in North Carolina, sitting on a rusty oil drum and watching fall leaves drift by, is incorporated in this book.

Momma's voice stopped my racing mind and brought me back into the moment. "Edward," she continued, "What if the Big But Syndrome becomes a huge hit? Are you sure you want to be known across the country as the guy who spends his time and energy worrying about the people's Big Buts?"

I said that nothing would make me happier.

"Well then go on and do it, Edward," Momma said. "I'll be very proud of you."

And she didn't say "but" once. Now that is a mother's love.

What you hold in your hands is my life and its lessons. I hope they help you lead a richer, fuller, happier life. I hope this book enlightens you, and relieves you of your own Big BUT.

Wishing you peace, prosperity, and a BUT-free lifestyle.

Eddie

Eddie Conner
Los Angeles, California

P.S. Throughout the book, you'll notice several illustrations of a donkey wearing a sandwich board. That's Ralph, the BUT donkey. Actually, he's not a donkey, he's an ass, which is what our BUTS can turn us into if we don't watch out. So be nice to Ralph the Ass, and remember: while Ralph may be stuck being an ass, you can always get rid of your BUT!

A Note to the Reader

This book is divided into two parts. The first discusses the epidemic of the Big BUT Syndrome and how we are habitually anal about the usage of our BIG BUTS. The second part covers the solutions and desires we have, while giving many Soul Tools you can use in your practical daily living.

It is my desire that one day soon, as you experience a mild problem, you will choose to utilize your human-soul potential first and put your old habits of thinking on the back burner. This alone will change your life in miraculous ways.

Enjoy.

Introduction

****

To believe is to be strong. Doubt cramps energy. Belief is power.

– Frederick William Robertson

Humans are the only species on this planet that contradicts desires with a variety of negative belief patterns. As a result, we are the only physical entities who can and do get ourselves caught in the trappings of the Big BUT Syndrome®.

According to the U.S. Census Bureau, the population in our country was 281,421,906 in the year 2000. Now, that's a lot of people in one location. It's no wonder the acreage we lived on as children has greatly reduced in size and tripled in value in such a short span of time.

Every minute, at least one million Americans are infected with the Big BUT Syndrome®, and every hour, the dreams of another five million people are extinguished.

Are you one of the millions of people working long hours to make your dreams a reality, BUT you can't seem to get where you want to go? Have you ever felt there was an invisible force holding you back from your long-awaited goals and aspirations? If so, you know what it feels like to be trapped in a contradicted vortex of hard work and frustration in which you realize you are not where you deserve to be in life.

Without realizing it, most adults talk in a contradictory way about the subjects that are most important to them. They express what they do and do not want in the same sentence. A common example of this behavior is when we hear people say things like, "I want a relationship, *but* most men are jerks." If I had a dime for every time I heard that sentence, I would have enough money in one year to buy a penthouse between Bill Gates and Donald Trump.

Another area of contrary desire is money. It is fascinating to observe people talking about lack of, absence of, and not-enough-of money in their lives. The desire for money is abundant enough, BUT the opposing belief to that desire is a poverty consciousness. In many ways, the same conflicted dynamic holds true with our personal beliefs around our careers.

When people seek advice from psychics, coaches, or therapists, they ask about the "Big Three" topics: Love, Money, and Career. These are the most talked about adult topics we engage in with the greatest desire and opposing negative emotion.

Mental note: the next time you are with friends or co-workers, listen and *feel* the frequency or energetic tone of the conversation. You will recognize the difference between hi-frequency and low-frequency dialogue immediately.

A hi-frequency tone ranges from a feel good, to a feel great, to an orgasmic sensation, while a low-frequency interaction ranges from complacency, to mild irritation, to a depressed energy tone.

As we talk about hi-frequency subjects, we attract more hi-frequency people, places, and situations. The same is true with low-frequency dialogues; as we discuss subjects that irritate us, we attract irritating people, places, and situations to us.

While chewing the fat with our buddies, we have a tendency to talk about, think about, and observe the things we do NOT want in life. We think we're talking about what we do want, because we're talking about subject matter that is important to us. However, more often than not, we're verbalizing and vibrating low-grade frequencies. For instance, during work how many times have we congregated at the water cooler to complain with our fellow associates about the neglect of upper management, pay cuts, mistreatment, or the fear of being laid off or worse, fired? In these moments, we are usually radiating a low frequency and observing more of what we do NOT want while we are talking about our job.

The frequency we emanate while communicating our thoughts or our spoken word is always a dead giveaway as to how we truly feel about the subject matter. If we are honestly talking about what we want, we should be feeling good about it–not bad.

Let's stick with relationships. Pretend you are single and out with good friends. The conversation turns to your desire to have a serious intimate relationship, someone to spend the rest of your life with. What is the first thing you and your friends talk about where love and finding the perfect someone to settle down with is concerned?

Did you notice how quickly and easily the conversation eroded into the old "learned" behavior that felt more low-frequency than hi-frequency? Just for fun, have you been in a conversation that sounded something like: "I want a relationship but, I don't want to waste any more time if he/she isn't the right one for me," or "The clock's ticking honey, I can't wait much longer, my eggs are drying up. Yikes, there goes another one! Quick, get me to the freezer!"?

Most adults spend more time imagining, pretending, daydreaming, fantasizing, and believing the impossibilities about our heartfelt, hi-frequency desires. We actively cancel out those positive needs and replace our pure desire with habitual problem-solving and troubleshooting patterns that we use to protect ourselves from repeating the same mistakes from our personal history. Or so we thought!

Where did we learn to contradict our desires?

We inherited this unseen habit of thought from authority figures while growing up. The fruit never falls far from the tree. For the most part, we are the byproducts of our ancestors, and we will more than likely follow in their footsteps. We must make a conscious decision to change our ancestral low-frequency patterns of contradiction to present-moment hi-frequency patterns of pure desire.

When we learn to love without contradicting love with worry, and when we consciously choose to appreciate the money in our pockets right now without complaining that it's not enough, our lives will change in miraculous ways.

The moment we lose our Big BUTs, we automatically emanate a series of pure, refined energy signals from within us to the heart and soul of the Universe. In return, the Universe can finally bring us what we do want instead of more of what we do not want.

I know all of us are here to create our personal greatness and to joyously carry that greatness in our heart, body language, and spirit. Tapping into this wellspring of bliss is easier to accomplish than we realize. All we have to do is start. As we say back home, there's a new day tomorrow and it ain't been touched yet.

It is my intention to offer you many **Soul Instruments** you can easily use in order to create your desired outcome with love, money, career, and other areas that are important to you.

Section One:
The Problem

1
Defining the Big BUT Syndrome®

Big: *Of considerable size, magnitude, large.*
But: *Contrary to expectation. But introduces a statement in opposition to what precedes it.*
Syndrome: *any complex of symptoms of the existence of an undesirable condition or quality.*

– American Heritage Dictionary

The Big BUT Syndrome®
Having considerable desire with a contradicted belief to that desire, which, over time, creates an unpleasant quality of life.

– Eddie Conner

Eleanor Roosevelt said, *"The future belongs to those who believe in the beauty of their dreams."*

As we have already established, the *Big BUT Syndrome*® is having a considerable desire with a contradicted belief to that desire, which, over time, creates an unpleasant quality of life.

In order to get a strong grasp on the essence of the Big BUT Syndrome® and how it negatively affects millions of us every second, it is important to amplify its emotional and intellectual aspects. On a booksmart level, the *American Heritage Dictionary* defines Desire and Belief as follows:

Desire: To express a wish for. To long for; want; crave.

Belief: Mental acceptance or conviction in the truth or actuality of something. Something believed or accepted as true.

On an intellectual and emotional level, each of us possesses both a desire (Emotion–more of a right-brain attribute) and a belief (Intellect–a left-brain attribute) about every subject known to humankind. Some subjects carry less desire and less belief than others.

First, there is desire (a hi-frequency emotion). We have a desire for unconditional love and for self-love. We have a desire for continued happiness and a desire for financial and spiritual prosperity in our lives and in the lives of those we love. We have a desire to be appreciated and respected and to be treated in an appropriate manner. We have a desire for good health, wellbeing, and wholeness, to name a few.

For each desire we hold, we also have a belief about that desire! Said belief is either in harmony with or opposed to our desire. If our belief and desire are in harmony, life feels great. And, if we have a desire with an opposing belief, our conscious left brain and subconscious right brain are, in essence, arguing with one another.

Next, there is belief (a perceived fact or truth). We have a belief the sun will continue shining its warm rays upon us. We have a belief there will always be plenty of oxygen to breathe.

We have a belief that hummingbirds are magical and otherworldly. Each listed belief is in harmony with the beliefs of the mass majority regarding the subject of hummingbirds, oxygen, and the sun's warm rays.

When we define *desire* and *belief,* giving examples of each, the definitions look and feel simple, *BUT* (pun intended) when we examine desire and belief together in a single subject that is extraordinarily important to us, like love, we frequently experience an emotional struggle rumbling in our gut, or what I like to call the **Solar Plexus Megaphone**®.

For an illustration of hi-frequency desire with an opposing belief, let's recap our previous paragraph on desire. As you read each statement listed below, feel free to write down or to say aloud your personal Belief about each desire.

> "I have a *desire* for unconditional love and self-love."
>
> "I have a *desire* for continued happiness and a *desire* for financial and spiritual prosperity in my life and in the lives of those I love."
>
> "I have a *desire* to be appreciated and respected and to be treated in an appropriate manner in all areas of my life."
>
> "I have a *desire* for good health, well-being, and wholeness."

Now, I would like to ask you how you are feeling about these statements of desire.

Is your desire for love/self-love in harmony with your existing belief that you can have it? Or do you have a negative belief that is opposing your desire for love? Do you possess hi-frequency desire for love/self-love with a low-frequency belief that you cannot have your desires fulfilled?

What is it about those important areas in life–where both our desire and beliefs are strong and often conflicting–that are causing our desire and our beliefs to put on their psychic boxing gloves and duke it out until the stronger of the two wins the fight? In many cases, the contradicted or opposing belief is usually the winner, thus leaving you and your desire losers in the game of love again.

At last, our big ole BUT enters the scenario. The reason the word BUT is one of my favorite words is its ability to virtually go unnoticed. It is practically invisible, not to mention it is one of the smallest and seemingly non-threatening words in the English language. Each time we use the word BUT, it is likened to the small stone in David's slingshot in the story of David and Goliath. That simple stone represents the power of our big BUT. Each time we put a single BUT in the slingshot of our opposing beliefs, it continues to bring down the giant empire of desire living inside us. BUT is almost always the crème sandwiched between the cookie of our desire and the cookie of our belief.

You could be experiencing a monumental avalanche of hi-frequency desire with an equal cataclysm of low-frequency belief in the same thought, sentence, or action. Quietly suspended between these two earth-shattering events is our itsy bitsy, teeny weenie, microscopic BUT, holding steadfast between our desire and our belief. BUT is contrary to expectation, and each BUT introduces a statement in opposition to whatever precedes it.

Let's apply our new knowledge. Since the subject of unconditional love for self and others is a conflicting and confusing area in life, most of my clients ask for clear examples of the Big BUT Syndrome® in this category.

Patti is a gorgeous thirty-something woman who raised her hand at a *"Create Your Soul Mate"* class I facilitate in the Los Angeles area. The few times she shared in class, it was obvious she was smart, articulate, and had a great sense of humor. With a smile in her voice, she simply stated, "I do want to fall madly in love again *BUT,* I'm afraid of getting hurt." The moment she finished speaking, a few others in our class gave her a series of high fives overlapped with a hearty round of "You Go Girl," capped off with some serious head bobbing. Um hmmm, gimme some!

It seemed 90 percent of the attendees were feeling the same contradiction, yet no one spoke of their deep desire or their fear that love hurts in such a direct, clear manner. Kudos to Patti for being the catalyst and sharing her honest emotions in a hi-frequency format.

Breaking down and identifying the bare bones of Patti's Big BUT Syndrome® looks a little something-like:

Patti's Desire: *"Wanting love"*
Patti's BUT: *"Opposes her desire for love"*
Patti's Belief: *"Fear of getting hurt"*

Like scores of people, Patti has a considerable desire to fall madly in love, coupled with a BUT belief that opposes her true emotional desire. Each time our BUT opposes our desire, it cancels out that desire. In other words, the big BUT cancels out whatever precedes it in our thoughts, speech, or emotions.

Have you ever been to a tractor pull? Or a better question would be, do you know what a tractor pull is? Growing up in North Carolina, tractor pulls were a permanent fixture at county fairs and such. So were monster truck rallies, car races on dirt tracks, NASCAR, and Sunday go-to-meeting church services where people spoke in tongues and kissed poisonous snakes on the lips. Do snakes have lips? I digress.

In essence, a tractor pull is a glorified game of tug-of-war in which school-aged children are replaced by tons of farm equipment, each piece of enormous machinery attempting to pull the weaker side into a manmade mud hole that could easily swallow the entire cast of *Hee Haw* and *The Beverly Hillbillies* put together.

Imagine two tractors, each with the exact amount of horsepower in their high-powered engines, facing in opposite directions. Both vehicles are equally equipped with gargantuan treaded tires and a sturdy chassis all geared up and ready to go.

We'll call tractor number one Desire. Desire represents Patti's desire to fall madly in love, and it is facing south. Tractor number two is Belief, representing Patti's belief she will get hurt when she finds love; Belief is facing north.

In every decent, honest-to-goodness tractor pull, there is a humble steel chain strategically hooked to the backside of each tractor. This chain is connected in such a manner that it evenly distributes the balance between both vehicles. In this way, no tractor has a jump on the other, and the tractor pull is fair and square. The chain represents the Big BUT Syndrome®.

Desire (Tractor One) and Belief (Tractor Two) are now in the final moments of preparation before competition. Both Desire and Belief rev their fire-breathing motors in a last-ditch attempt to psych out and intimidate the other. The crowd in the stadium grows restless, probably from too much caffeine.

Two eager pit crews of burly men wearing flannel shirts and leather belts with snazzy sayings engraved on them like, "Hi, I'm Charlie Horse," swarm between the ferocious treaded monsters preparing each for the main event. A referee motions the pit crews to finish their task seconds before he waves the starting flag.

Desire and Belief accelerate against one another as Bubba, the crew leader, hooks up the steel chain, which is capable of effortlessly withstanding up to three tons of force. The anxious crowd in the stadium leaps to its feet, screaming as the referee drops the starting flag in a downward motion–and they're off.

From a bird's-eye view in the stadium, it is a sensory marvel to experience the aroma of diesel fuel smoking from beneath raging machines, hear engines whining, and watch as multi-ton machines buck against one another in a challenge to the finish. Mud flies in every direction.

At full acceleration, both engines scream and grind in a dead heat fury as Desire and Belief jerk and jolt back and forth at an exhausting pace. The steel chain holds the tension between each tractor, rarely, if ever, giving either much slack in any direction.

With mud flying and the crowd roaring, Desire gains a few inches to the south and in a second, Belief has gained a microscopic lead to the north. Desire's engine is howling, its tires gripping the mud to create forward movement.

The steel chain continues to hold the tractor tug-of-war in perfect balance. Desire is able to pull Belief a good three feet in the direction of the foreboding mud hole. And just when the crowd thought Desire was locked in and could do no wrong, Belief hunkered down, scrawling and carving the earth like an electric knife in a Thanksgiving turkey.

Bucking and pulsing forward, Desire and Belief pull against one another for the next ten minutes before the referee calls an end to the non-winning twosome, both covered in mud and exasperated from their efforts. In the end, the crowd is irritated to see Desire and Belief are pretty much sitting in the exact same spot they started, give or take the few inches. Belief has managed to pull Desire closer toward the mud hole.

Technically speaking, neither tractor has won, because neither tractor hit the mud hole. Just the same, it is Belief that has managed to pull Desire a touch closer to the dark, muddy pit. After all their effort, hard work, and exhausting planning, they are both basically back at square one.

Bubba quickly dismantles the unbreakable chain from both vehicles and drops it to the ground, liberating Desire to go any direction it chooses and releasing Belief to freely roam.

It is the nearly invisible, non-threatening chain that binds a person's desire and belief together in the tug-of-war of our mind and emotions. When we make the decision to do so, we disengage from our Big BUT, and the three-ton steel chain confining us simply drops to the ground, freeing us to desire what we choose to desire and own the beliefs that compliment and harmonize with that desire.

The common denominator holding Patti's desire and belief in gridlock is a simple steel chain called the Big BUT Syndrome®.

Watching the tractor pull, there is no comparison between the tractors' loud motors and the single thread of chain binding Patti's desire and belief together in a stronghold. However, as powerful as her desire is to fall madly in love, it is her fear– a.k.a. *belief* that–she will get hurt "again" if she falls in love that restricts her desire for love.

The BUT Chain that binds our desires and beliefs is virtually unseen and often unheard, because we think the word BUT, we say the word BUT, and act upon the word BUT so often that it goes unnoticed, unseen, and unheard where our five physical senses are concerned. As in the commotion of the tractor pull, all eyes and ears in the audience are fixated on the tractor of Desire or the tractor of Belief fighting against each other while hardly anyone in the stands pays much attention to the BUT Chain that binds Patti's desire and belief in a contradictory knot.

It is our sixth sense, our emotional sense, that perceives the contradiction in our solar plexus when we desire and fear something in the same breath. It is our **Soul Electricity**® that gingerly tugs at our inner guidance system to remind us in a loving manner that using low-frequency thoughts with low-frequency vocabulary (**Vibratory Vocabulary**®) does not serve our highest desire for good.

When we kill our desires, we are, in essence, killing ourselves. We are pulling ourselves further away from a natural state of being. Our birthright is to create feel-good things through our hi-frequency desires and hi-frequency intellect.

Desire makes the world, the Universe, go round. Our belief or justification that we cannot have what we desire is what stops the desire from creating a manifestation on our behalf. To desire love, financial freedom, or the perfect profession is normal; it is our birthright.

The next time you have a considerable desire for a love relationship, money, or a better career, which tractor will you choose to put hi-frequency fuel into? Will you choose to put your energy into the tractor of Desire *"I want to fall madly in love,"* or will you choose the tractor with an opposing belief to your desire, *"I don't want to get hurt again"?* Or, will you choose both?

You may be saying, "Of course I would put my hi-frequency fuel into my desire." BUT, I'll also bet that when you consciously focus on love, money, or career, you will automatically (and innocently) flip back to your old habits, those low-frequency historical beliefs.

Remember to drop your three-ton BUT Chain so your little red tractor has the free will to travel anywhere its heart desires.

Will you unconsciously pick up the steel chain that opposes your desire and get caught in the mental and emotional tractor pull of life? Or, will you appreciate yourself and bask in the Soul Electricity of your heartfelt desire, ignoring outdated beliefs and the Bubbas of life carrying BUT Chains?

As physically focused awareness, we will always operate from a core desire, and we will always have a belief about that desire. Our greatest victory as human consciousness is to own our core desire with pure belief in perfect unison. This brilliant combustion point of consciousness is complete freedom. In essence, this unison is the heart and soul of evolution moving our planet forward.

> **Desire** is the emotion/feeling we crave.
>
> **BUT** opposes or cancels desire (steel chain).
>
> **Belief** is our intellectual thought accepted as true.

The moral of our story is: Don't be a Bubba sporting BUT linkage.

2
Proceed With Caution:
BUT Zones Ahead

BIG BUT Zones are subjects we observe silently or aloud that cause us to contradict our desires with opposing beliefs to those desires. For example: "I want to go to my high school reunion, *BUT* first I need to lose 15 pounds." In other words, we talk about our desire for lightness while also talking about and feeling overweight. In essence, we are fence-sitting about body image.

The main areas that we have a tendency to display consistent contradiction in are love, money, and career. Other BUT Zones in which we frequently send mixed signals are:

> Body image, health, and weight
> Sexuality and sensuality
> Family, friends, and co-workers
> Traffic or commute
> Religion and structured education
> Aging, death, and dying
> Food (When was the last time you ate something decadent without feeling guilty about it?)
> Did I mention family? (There's always some serious BUT action happening in the family department.)

ASK YOURSELF:

1-In which areas do you have the biggest BUT, and why?

2-What is my personal self-talk about the area (s) I chose above?

3-What would I like to hear in my mind?

Just for fun, put on your psychic stopwatch. Pick a BUT Zone topic listed above that you personally have problems with. Once you have chosen your topic, begin talking aloud about that topic, and once you contradict the topic with a negative belief, stop the watch and see how long (or how short) a time you spoke before you were infected with the BIG BUT Syndrome. You might surprise yourself.

For example: Let's say you choose Body Image. How long can you write or speak about your body without verbally, mentally, or emotionally saying, thinking, or feeling bad vibes about the amazing machine and mechanics we call the human body?

Isn't it phenomenal what our bodies do every one hundredth of a second? Our hearts pump blood to keep us going while sending thought waves to every atom, cell, and molecule in the visible *and* invisible worlds on a daily basis–all without our giving it a single thought.

Like everything in life, our bodies respond to our invisible thoughts and feelings about it. They cannot do otherwise. If we send our bodies low-frequency feelings, they will respond back to us in a low-frequency manner. And, when we send our body hi-frequency energy, it responds accordingly, giving us back hi-frequency results.

Think about the weight epidemic in our country at the moment. This may shock you, *BUT*, the weight we are wearing is not a direct result of the food we are eating too much of or the lack of exercise in our lives. The weight we are wearing on our bodies is a result of how we *feel* about the food we're eating and how we *feel* about not getting the exercise. We are spending more time and low-frequency emotion on what we DON'T WANT about our bodies than we spend appreciating the absolute miracles our bodies perform every single second of our lives!

If you're not happy with your body, chances are you're focusing on the problem area and not looking at the dozens, even hundreds, of areas in which your body is functioning perfectly–and looking extraordinary, too. Remember, if you don't like your existing body image, it's a direct result of how you've been feeling about it over time. After years of talking about and pointing out the negative parts of your body, the negative points have become bigger.

My good friend Janice tells me she thinks the weight she feels on her body today is a result of how she felt about her body a few years ago. And the weight she felt on her body a few years ago was due to the way she thought and felt about her body five years earlier than that.

Seriously? Well, butter my butt and call me a biscuit.

A great illustration of what I'm referring to comes in the form of old photographs. I'm in my 50s now. Anytime I see old pictures of myself in my 40s, I gasp in disbelief at how slim and trim I was. Of course at the time the picture was taken, I thought or felt heavier and less attractive than I actually was. Talk about not living in the present moment–duh!

Then, I see pictures of myself in my 30s! What the heck was I thinking back then? Again, in my 20s, I was quick to point out my flaws and shortcomings, and today, standing in my 55 year-old body looking back at me then, I easily recognize my invisible negative thoughts of insecurity and self criticism that have unconditionally followed me through the years. In other words, my body (as all things do) is simply responding to my low or hi-frequency thoughts about it.

Aren't you ready to be standing on the backside of negativity? I know I am. Take a brief moment to recap your BUT Zone areas in history. It seems the older we get, the more intense our personal BUT Zones become and the harder it is to crawl out from under our conflicted beliefs about ourselves.

3

Symptoms of the Big BUT Syndrome®

Breaking down the word *disease* simply means there is a dis-ease in the vibration of a subject we have chosen to focus on. When I think about Celine Dion singing her heart out in her Las Vegas show, I feel an easy flow in my thoughts and emotions. As I shift my thoughts and feelings to desperately trying to complete two major deadlines in one afternoon, I feel a distinct DIS-ease within myself.

When we continue this level of dis-ease for long periods of time, it eventually diminishes our quality of life. Over time, we will experience one or more of the following symptoms:

Feeling Tired	Lack of Energy	Jealousy
Indecision	Hurt Feelings	Why Me Syndrome
Frustration	Poor Me Syndrome	Needy, Sucky
Blurry Thinking	Disease to Please	Not Good Enough
Irritability	Pessimism	Feeling Not Seen
Over Thinking	Whining	Feeling Not Heard
Creating Chaos	Complaining	Imbalanced Ego
Manipulation	Negative Comparison	Directionless
Self-critical	Critical of Others	Seeking Approval
Self-hatred	Self-loathing	Complaining

Emotionally holding on to any of these low-frequency attributes for any amount of time will slow down and eventually stop our heartfelt desires. Getting ourselves trapped in this low-frequency quicksand tricks us into turning our backs on our authentic soul power and hypnotizes us into focusing our attention on what we can physically see and hear in the moment.

Our dreams and desires fall into the dark, grim recesses of the BUT Crack of Life, trapped from the light of our whole soul-self.

If we are not careful, we may habitually fall into a dark cycle of believing the life we are living will not change. When we continue to observe the hardships and shortcomings life unconditionally gives us, we will absolutely attract more of the same. I have not met a person yet who can talk, think, or observe negative thoughts for longer than a few moments without possessing low negative vibrations as a result. Conversely, I have not met anyone who focuses on hi-frequency thoughts or events who stil lives in consistent poverty.

Way back when I was only knee high to a grasshopper, I noticed these two dominant personality types. They are:

1. Hi-frequency Personalities = Prosperity Consciousness
2. Low-frequency Personalities = Poverty Consciousness

I deliberately chose the spelling "Hi" over the traditional spelling of the word "High." As we learn more about how words themselves carry an invisible vibration, we will see *and feel* an elevated vibratory output in some words and a lower, lethargic frequency in others. "Hi" literally looks and feels like an invisible, rapid-fire, effective laser point of focus; whereas "high" spelled traditionally looks and feels physically focused, more real, and more normal. It literally feels like a slower frequency of energy is pulsating from it.

Hi-frequency Personalities see the glass as half full. They are more balanced in their right and left-brain transmissions while moving through life operating from their hearts and self-confidence, and standing in the light of their crown chakra. In short, Hi-frequency Personalities are multidimensional and multi sensory, operating in the world through their soul-self while in perfect sync with their physical, human personality.

Low-frequency Personalities see the glass as half empty. They complain about the quality of the water in the glass, predicting the glass will surely break and the water will disappear to boot! Low-frequency people are not good problem solvers as much as they are excellent at discovering new problems in their lives and yours, whether you ask them or not.

They are excellent at shining in a crisis without realizing they themselves created the crisis in which to shine. They operate predominately from the left brain and see the world through their physical eyes more often than they allow themselves to dream desires from their whole-soul perspective.

In short, they choose, more often than not, to focus on the problems and shortcomings in their lives. They look at the world through limited vision, without honoring the heart and emotional dreams their souls are whispering to them.

The symptoms our Big BUTS trap us in are extreme and chaotic, riddled with hi-frequency desires that are body-slammed to the mat by the WWF of opposing beliefs that we cannot have what we want. Over time, our mind and physical body take a beating from a gamut of invisible feelings rampaging through us with the greatest of dis-ease.

Are you mostly hi-frequency or low-frequency? Perhaps you are a little bit of both. In the next few days, choose to observe as many things as you can that make you feel good. When you are feeling good, put on your thinking C.A.P.

> *C*elebrate and
> *A*ppreciate moments you feel hi-frequency. This in turn
> *P*erpetuates more hi-frequency manifestations. Then begin the cycle again!

4
The OVAL Mirror® of Life

Everyone is familiar with the mean old witch in *Snow White*. The witch stands in her huge castle before her magic mirror and recites the famous question, "Mirror, mirror on the wall, who's the fairest of them all?" In the story, until Snow White comes along, the enchanted mirror always reassures the witch that she is, indeed, the fairest.

Ah, to have a magic mirror in the 21st century; how lovely that would be! To feel guilt-free about having our favorite Ben and Jerry's ice cream at midnight and still have the willpower to stand in front of a magic mirror the next morning without staring at ourselves as if alien seedpods took up permanent residence in our bodies. "What thighs?" The mirror might sweetly say.

When observing ourselves in the mirror for longer than a few minutes, why do most of us have a habit of searching for imperfections and flaws like a heat-seeking missile honing in on its doomed target? Why don't we see our beauty?

It seems we have digressed to, "Is my butt too big for these jeans?" instead of looking for the good. And what of the beauty we possess inside? The compassion, kindness, patience–where are those beautiful aspects of the self celebrated? When did we start believing it was more appropriate to talk about our flaws and imperfections rather than our beauty? When did we begin hiding our true light under a bushel and casting pearls to the swine of our negative focus?

How many times have you stood in front of a mirror semi-horrified as you saw your reflection, wanting to scream, "Mirror, mirror on the wall, don't make me fling you down the hall"? I think it is safe to say many of us have mirror drama in our lives. Whether it is blaming ourselves for giving into that midnight ice cream indulgence, not making it to the gym, or cursing our genetics, standing naked in front of a mirror can bring up our low-frequency personalities, causing us to feel bad about ourselves.

Because of my fascination with human nature verses the mirror, (kinda sounds like a wrestling match, doesn't it?), I have created the OVAL Mirror®.

The OVAL Mirror of life is one of my favorite tools to use in explaining how we manifest the lives we are living. Since childhood, I have believed all humans have a soul and because of our souls, we do not die. I feel all people are born knowing we are souls being human first and humans being spiritual second. I am certain we came from a nonphysical realm that is composed of unconditional love and pure light. From this expanded state of consciousness, we choose to be born into the earth plane and live a physical experience.

Because all souls are nonphysical energy in action, designed in source energies likeness, we are 100 percent invisible energy. Once we decide to float from nonphysical energy into a human form, our 100 percent invisible consciousness becomes 99.99% nonphysical, leaving the other .01% to live and function in a physical body. In essence, we are invisibly connected to the nonphysical world through hi-frequency umbilical cords from our Human Intuitive Intellect® and to the heart and soul of the Universe.

As with all mirrors, the OVAL Mirror of everlasting life reflects everything that is in it. Other three-dimensional mirrors reflect only our physical personalities. BUT the OVAL Mirror reflects whatever we are vibrating *on an emotional level.* This extraordinary mirror gives back everything we are vibrating

24/7. If we are vibrating low-frequency emotions, we get back low-frequency results. As we choose to focus on positive thoughts, feelings, and memories, the OVAL Mirror unconditionally reflects back to us feel-good physical realities.

I believe every soul, in the process of being born, stood in front of the OVAL Mirror before being physically incarnated. Because we are still connected to our soul's essence, even while living in human bodies, we have unlimited access to the knowledge and energy of All That Is. I like the idea that our higher self and oversoul stood with us in front of the OVAL Mirror before we came to Earth. Together, they read with us the engraving on the OVAL Mirror's ornate frame. The frame reads:

> What I feel is what I get.
> When I choose to feel good,
> I receive good things.
> When I choose to feel bad,
> I receive bad things.
> It is always my choice,
> Because . . . (repeats)

Because the frame is an infinite, eternal symbol, the carved words wrap around the mirror in a manner that caused our soul to read them until the frequency of these words vibrated so high, so fast, and so pure that every cell in our human bodies was framed with the message that our invisible thoughts, invisible feelings, and invisible vibrations created our earthly realities.

Why is the mirror shaped like an oval? So we would remember how we create our lives on earth with the assistance and power of our invisible, nonphysical Soul Self. Simply stated, O.V.A.L. means that whatever:

We	**O**bserve	causes us to vibrate. What
We	**V**ibrate	
We	**A**ttract.	And what we attract
We	**L**ive	

Someone once said misery loves company, and we must believe that. As humans, we have a consistent habit of focusing on what we don't want. We talk about what we don't want, how it feels to have what we don't want, and how unfair it is that we are living what we don't want. We spend more time complaining and activating enormous BUTS instead of dreaming and activating enormous DESIRES. The OVAL effect below gives us an idea of how we attracted the life we are living today:

When we	**O**BSERVE	the BIG BUT
We then	**V**IBRATE	the BIG BUT
Then we	**A**TTRACT	the BIG BUT
Finally, we	**L**IVE	the BIG BUT

Take a moment to let this sink in. If you are not living your highest desires, then recognize that you must change your thoughts and feelings–and the sooner the better! When we **choose** a feel-good decision to play with the miraculous power the Universe affords us, we can shift our focus on an internal level to create our external reality. Our old, habitual, low-frequency thoughts turn into a new consciousness of hi-frequency thoughts and feelings.

When we	**O**BSERVE	the Solution
We then	**V**IBRATE	the Solution
Then we	**A**TTRACT	the Solution
Finally, we	**L**IVE	the Solution

Each of us has the free will to choose his or her thoughts and feelings. We have free will about what we choose to observe. It has always been our choice. We can choose the old, low-frequency thoughts, or we can choose the new desires with supportive beliefs to our desires. It is your choice, your decision.

Low-frequency =

    My butt looks big in these jeans.

    My lover will not take out the trash.

    I am not getting paid what I am worth.

Hi-frequency =

> Hey, my jeans still fit!
>
> Isn't it great, Mike's busy doing what he loves?
>
> I feel like a million bucks today! I'm asking for a raise.

It takes a strong, spiritually centered person to stand in front of a mirror, especially the OVAL Mirror, and make a point to consciously observe his or her positive aspects. To appreciate ourselves unconditionally and applaud our current successes and our future dreams is a gift we can give ourselves. It feels great, and it actually helps us achieve our goals and dreams. It can take extraordinary effort to stand amid the conflicts in your physical life experience and choose to observe beauty in your mind's eye, instead of the dramas being played out around you.

Fixin' the Big BUT Syndrome will take some practice. Play with conscious choice and remember the OVAL Mirror of life. Unlock your full human-soul potential by using your free will. The free will to choose our thoughts is the greatest present we have in our Present Moment experience. Don't waste it; think a beautiful thought right now!

"Mirror, mirror in my Soul, thanks for making me feel whole."

5

The 1-2-3's of Your B-U-T

As your personal BUT Guide, it is my duty to steer you as far away from America's real crack problem as I can. By the end of this book, you will be more than able to kick your own BIG BUT. Utilizing the 1-2-3's is a lighthearted way to rise above the BUT habit of having hi-frequency desire with an opposing low-frequency belief to that desire. Whenever you feel a BIG BUT creeping into your intellectual and emotional awareness, allow the new you to incorporate this simple hi-frequency recipe for success.

> **B** is for Be Aware of the BUT
> **U** is for Undo the BUT Belief
> **T** is for Transcend and Begin Again!

Step1 – Be Aware

Be aware of the moments you contradict your desires and beliefs in the same frame of thought. More often than not, out of old, low-frequency habits, these BUTS slip through the crack of your consciousness, and before you realize it, you are back to the old past-tense aspect of your personality, recycling your old way of thinking and feeling about life.

Being aware that the Big BUT Syndrome is actively holding your dreams at bay makes you more responsible for allowing your good to manifest. Being conscious that you are using BUT language with BUT emotion does not mean to be self-critical and hard on yourself. It simply means that being aware of your Big BUT habit NOW will get you closer to living a life filled with ease, not DIS-ease.

Step 2 – Undo BUT Beliefs

Undo it. Once you catch yourself being stuck in the trappings of Big BUT behavior, activate Step 1, **Be Aware**, and immediately implement Step 2, **Undo BUT Beliefs**, with a feel-good frequency. Hi-frequencies always feel good to you. Things like laughing, jokes, humor, music, and affirmations are a few tools to use while undoing this old BUT pattern. The more you feel good, the faster your Big BUT is defused, leaving you powerfully in the flow of life.

Step 3 – Transcend and Begin Again!

Transcend and begin again, utilizing the power and strength of your Soul Electricity. Transcend the normal human belief and go beyond, exceed, and rise above the norm in order to live BUT-Free. This amplifies your desires in a high, pure manner. Transcend your old BUT Belief by reframing your initial Big

BUT statement to fit your hi-frequency desire. Use your Soul Electricity to harness good thoughts, good feelings, and a great outcome.

Choose the power of positive focus. Focus + Feelings = Reality. Reframe, Retrain, and Revive your life by utilizing the 1-2-3's of your B-U-T.

Let's recap Janice's amazing and accurate observation about weight and body image from the BUT *Zones* chapter, while weaving the 1-2-3's of our B-U-T and the OVAL Mirror into a lovely feel-good tapestry. First, we'll reassess our OVAL acronym with: Whatever we

> **O**bserve in life causes us to
> **V**ibrate. What we vibrate causes us to
> **A**ttract and what we attract, we will
> **L**ive.

This OVAL Mirror is an invisible hi-frequency mirror responding and reflecting our thoughts and feelings back to us. For example: if we don't like our bodies in our 20s, this thought and vibration is reflected back to us over the years until it manifests on our person. If we feel ten pounds heavier than we'd like, we are observing a problem that makes us feel bad.

As we observe low-frequency problems that make us feel bad, we are in that exact one hundredth of a second vibrating, attracting, and eventually living the problem we are observing. And this invisible cycle continues for eternity.

Though I was slightly self-critical of my body in my 20s and 30s, it is easy to see how I created (along with much of the nation) half a lifetime of low-frequency attributes about body image, and today, I AM living the base of that vibration. In other words, my weight is roughly ten pounds up and down depending on my feelings, or vibratory output.

Today, when I sense those old familiar thoughts and feelings creeping into my awareness, I implement **Step One** and I choose to **Be Aware** that I'm riding out a BUT wave of negativity.

I take responsibility for thinking thoughts like, "I always feel ten pounds heavier than I want to be." By taking responsibility, I am not blaming the pulled-pork with chicken and dumplings, or ho' cake with mashed potatos and gravy. The last time I checked in with myself, these food items have never jumped off the table and into my mouth without my consent. Well, except for that one time on a cruise ship during the midnight dessert buffet. And trust me when I say it wasn't a pretty picture!

I literally stop and **Become Aware** that I am vibrating a contradicted desire that is low frequency and springboard into **Step Two and Undo** the **BUT Belief.**

Undoing the old belief is easier to achieve when you employ what I call your Soul Electric attributes. Soul Electricity is always something that makes you feel like a million bucks! And each moment you choose to feel great, you are no longer radiating a contradicted signal that is sabotaging you.

Awareness is a powerful thing. Now that you are aware your hi-frequency thoughts and feelings in the OVAL Mirror of life can change your experience simply by observing feel-good subjects, you will likely loose that old five (or ten) pounds of low-frequency momentum that you're wearing on your body more easily.

Today, if I accidentally fall into a BIG BUT sinkhole, I immediately begin observing things around me that are working brilliantly on my behalf. I appreciate my home, the houseplants, the flower gardens, the horses, the sunny California weather, talking with mom, my clean and organized office, the hummingbirds outside my window, or the fact that my car starts each time I crank it. And if that doesn't feel like quite enough, I play my favorite music and dance around my house like a big ole fool! *She's a maniac, maniac on the floor* . . . I love the movie *Flashdance* and the soundtrack too!

These are hi-frequency attributes that empower me into being aware and undoing my BUT Beliefs. And now, you are ready to dive head first into Step 3–

Transcend and Begin Again. One of my favorite spiritual principles is that our Focus + Feelings = Reality. It's an abbreviated OVAL Mirror effect.

It feels wonderful to me that my focused thoughts and feelings (invisible attributes) create my physical reality every second of my life. As a result of this basic lesson, I make a deliberate decision to direct my focus toward everything physical and invisible that feels hi-frequency and fabulous to me.

Speaking of body image, another preferred thing I do while I am out and about in the world is to appreciate people with great bodies. Men and women who are toned, slim, trim, muscular, in shape, confident, comfortable, and at ease in their bodies–especially as they move through their day sporting their flattering wardrobe. I use this appreciation technique as my daily **"Feel Good Free-For-All"** ritual. Do this some time. It truly works.

It feels good to feel good! Any moment we choose the luxury and gift of feeling good, we are living–in that exact moment–a BUT-Free existence. Truth be told, that is all we want anyway, isn't it? We want our desires to come to us without the negative backlash we've created for ourselves in the past. Granted, we created the negativity unconsciously with our BUT vocabulary and BUT beliefs, and today, we can start fresh in the *NOW*.

I encourage you to change your life by changing your focus. Choose hi-frequency Soul Electricity over your old programming. Live in the present moment and allow the gift your NOW experience brings to you. And when the BIG BUT sneaks through the cracks of your consciousness, joyously apply a teeny weenie 1-2-3 and blast your B-U-T into orbit.

6

The Truth about Yeah, BUTS

Can I say that I love Chellie Campbell? For the last 257 days I have carried her book, *The Wealthy Spirit*: *Daily Affirmations for Financial Stress Reduction,* with me all across the country, and I tell everyone about her book. How do I know it has been 257 days? Because her book is broken down into three segments per day: first is the quote, second is a simple story, and third is a daily affirmation that marries the quote and story together. Simply stated, you read one page a day and practice the affirmations for ten minutes. In a sense, each page is an absolute Energetic Multiple Orgasmic Combustion Point, and I am grateful to my friend Ellen for suggesting it to me. Thanks, girl!

I was co-facilitating a retreat in Grand Rapids, Michigan, when I read page 38. It was entitled "Yeah, Buts." The moment I read the title, I gasped aloud.

The chapter illustrates how damaging "yeah, buts" are to ourselves and to the people who offer to help us solve problems in our careers and personal lives. Chellie writes, "'Yeah buts' have a very negative psychological effect on the person trying to help. They've just been rejected, essentially told that their advice is no good, inappropriate, or doesn't work."

She continues with, "You will find yourself getting richer and happier when you eliminate the words 'yeah, but' from your vocabulary. Instead of 'Yeah, but' say, 'Thank you for the suggestion! Help me see how I can apply that to my situation.'"

I was also thrilled when I reached chapter 68, which is entitled "Stopping Points." Here, Chellie provides 15 wonderful examples of the "yeah, buts" with easy exercises to rid them from your life.

Yeah, BUTS block our good, suffocate our power, and disillusion us with low-frequency negativity. When you are spewing "Yeah, BUTS," employ the 1-2-3's of the B-U-T or the AND Avalanches. Call upon the Big BUT Stand-ins or the Punctuation Shields and if all else fails, utilize my favorite BUT Blaster of all and Laugh your BUT off!

I can honestly say *The Wealthy Spirit* has changed my perspective and given me many new tools to use on my path of spiritual growth and financial stress reduction.

7
The Infamous Invisi-BUTS

Famed Choreographer and American modern dancer, Martha Graham said, "Misery is a communicable disease." I feel the same about Invisi-BUTS.

Invisible BUTS are silent killers surrounding us like ghosts we cannot see or hear. We can only sense these invisible contradictions of energy influencing us deeper and deeper still into the dark crevices of the low-frequency disconnection from our Soul Self.

The obvious BUTS are the ones we think, speak, and take action toward. We hear ourselves using BUT Vocabulary, and more often than not, we are pretty much conscious of our basic emotional belief about areas that are important to us. Actually, we are so conditioned to using the standard BUT in our thoughts and spoken word that we do not pay much attention to feeling bad when we do utilize the "B" word.

Why have we conditioned ourselves to think it is normal to feel bad and habitually focus on negative, low-frequency thoughts and things?

Invisible BUTS are sneaky. They do not fight fair, and they love hitting us below the belt.

Invisi-BUTS travel in packs with the intention of penetrating one small, negative belief inside us first, then releasing the rabid pack of BUTS on us next, each one ripping our desires to shreds. Before we know it, we are surrounded by numerous ghosts biting us with low-frequency fangs over and over until we begin to believe we cannot have our deserved desires.

A typical low-frequency BUT Belief is: "I need more money, *BUT* I don't know how else to get it."

I met Karen Moriuchi while touring in Hawaii. She is an amazing teacher and an exceptional guide with endless knowledge about the Big Island's folklore and history. Between sights, Karen and I were semi-attacked by wild cocks and frightened by a bearded hermit wielding motorized farm equipment. We nicknamed him The Hawaiian Chainsaw Massacre as we laughed and ran for our lives from chainsaws and wild cocks. *BUT* that's another story for another time.

A master practitioner of NeuroLinguistic Programming (NLP), Karen taught me that BUT is an eraser word. Karen said, "Our brain negates and does not consider what we said before the BUT. I think our brain hears the BUT and then it does not pay attention to what came before it because the information after it is usually contradictory . . . so the brain drops one part of our thought."

In the illustration above, the word BUT erases the desire for money and puts the emphasis on the opposing belief to our "now erased" desire! All the weight now lands on the second half of the sentence, which is the low-frequency belief, "I don't know how else to get it."

The Big BUT Breakdown happens when we talk about our desires and BUT beliefs in the same sentence.

Desires + BUT = zero results. The desire is erased, and the BUT stands next to our negative belief. Before we realize it, our Big BUT has taken the bride-zilla of negative belief. That is one honeymoon I don't want to visualize. Yikes.

Unlike their more obvious, outspoken cousin, Invisi-BUTS seem to come from out of nowhere. Using the same category of money, the invisible BUT would take a quiet, silent approach. Here's an example: You're excited because it is payday, and you're ready for a long weekend away from work. You receive your paycheck and swiftly deposit it into the bank, keeping $40 cash for the weekend.

After work, you drive home, check your mailbox, and see them waiting for you. The bills, bills, and more bills piled up in your mailbox, face down, patiently waiting to surprise you. Without warning, your appreciation for your paycheck and the cash in your pocket quickly disappears into the pang of negative emotion in your solar plexus. Suddenly, you believe you have more money going out than coming in. Now, worry has set in, followed by an army of negative, low-frequency thoughts like, "How am I ever going to get out of this financial mess," or, "I have to find another area to cut back in until I get my credit cards paid off."

Before we realize it, every dollar in our pocket is not nearly enough to get us out of financial trouble. Then we forget to appreciate the gift of the money we possess and instead replace our appreciation of the money we have with the worry-zilla-itis!

Once the first Invisi-BUT penetrates our thin shield, it's much like hitting a hornets' nest with a short stick. It opens the door to swarms of negative thought patterns that put us in a self-inflicted cocoon of low-frequency crap. And that's not pretty.

To prevent Invisi-BUT infestation, you want to choose to observe things that uplift, nurture, and serve you. You want to think the thoughts and dream the dreams that enhance your visions and aspirations.

When you feel a low-frequency pang of negative feeling creeping into your Solar Plexus Megaphone,

STOP and shift that low frequency into something higher and more electric that truly honors your new mission statement to win in the game of life,

AND to feel good about feeling good,

AND to share that overflowing wellness with yourself,

AND others around you as frequently as you can.

8

Big BUT Understudies and Stand-ins on the Stage of Life

Everything has a family of energetic thought associated with it, and our teeny weenie BUT is no exception. Everything seen and unseen has an electromagnetic energy that supports and sustains it.

The more attention we give something, the stronger its lifespan. And the measure of influence we give it always affects our lives in a positive or negative manner. If we give attention to a negative thought, it will affect our lives negatively. BUT, if we give attention to a positive thought, our lives will be affected positively.

By attention, I am referring to thought, emotion, imagination, worry, concern, action, belief, and desire–especially contradicted desire.

Surely all BUTs must need a break from time to time from this production we call life. It is a full-time job for one BUT to run around opposing nearly every desire we have from morning to night, since the first day we were born.

When our overworked BUT finally gets a break from its exhausting show business schedule we call life, it calls on a handful of temporary replacements, or stand-ins (i.e., synonyms) that wait patiently in the wings for their big break in the spotlight.

As the Big BUT Syndrome® exits the stage of our daily life from shear exasperation, or takes a vacation from its duties, it summons one of its understudies to step out in its place. These temporary stand-ins will hold down the fort until our BUT steps back in, stealing the show from its less effective apprentices.

Who are these struggling Big BUT wannabes, desperately waiting in the wings for their big chance in the spotlight? They are none other than the infamous Big BUT synonyms:

| However | Still | Instead |
| Yet | Nevertheless | |

BUT Synonyms introduce, to varying degrees, a statement in opposition to what precedes them. All Big BUT vocabulary has a watered-down, low frequency about it. This includes the less visible apprentices listed above. Big BUTS are contradicted thought patterns that originate in our conscious thinking, then are immediately packed away into the storehouse of our subconscious mind where they live forever. Our Big BUTS are seen as smart, physical safety nets designed to caution us from repeating old, familiar patterns or from getting our feelings hurt again.

Not getting overly excited about important matters and being careful not to dream bigger than our means has become one of the most irresponsible habits we, as adults, have fallen into. Somewhere along life's journey, we slowly begin to believe certain people who encouraged us to dream only as high as our credit card limits. These are the same people who taught us that worrying about money, love, or career was responsible adult behavior. In essence, worrying about anything that causes us to feel negative emotion only brings us more things in life to feel negative emotion about. In other words, worrying is NOT a responsible adult act.

Desiring and believing we have the ability to create whatever we want is a Universal Truth. It is an unspoken reality gifted from our Soul Self to our Human Self that lives inside every cell, atom, and molecule of our being that we brought with us when we were born.

We are Souls first and humans second. We choose to come from the nonphysical expression of our being and into a physical body. Upon arriving on Earth in these bodies, we begin expressing our pure Human Soul potential. We are literally Universal Oneness in physical human form. We have the unlimited, unconditional love, guidance, and support from the Universe to experience greatness for ourselves and help others experience their greatness.

When we reach deep in our hearts, we can feel an eager, enthusiastic, animated, electric, brilliant, innocent, all-knowing, loving, and spiritually prosperous genius that has a unique gift to share with the world. All of us are born feeling and knowing our true attributes. Nothing can stop our ability to co-create with the Universe on the behalf of our desires, except us.

The only thing standing between our desires is OUR OWN self-inflicted Big BUT Belief that we cannot have our desires fulfilled.

Each BUT Stand-In belongs to low-frequency vocabularies that evoke low-frequency feelings that will create low-frequency manifestations. There is no **Soul Electricity** or high, pure frequency within the walls of these words. These words are vibratory family members of our Big BUT. Our BIG BUT Stand-ins live under the umbrella of the BUT.

A shining example of *Stand-Ins* comes to mind in the guise of a lovely lady I've affectionately nicknamed Ms. Hills. Beverly Hills that is, swimming pools, movie stars. Can't you hear the 70s sitcom music twanging away in your subconscious as the distinguished male commentator announces the arrival of The Beverly Hillbillies in television sets in living rooms across the country?

The Soul Mate Class was held in Los Angeles and was filled with enthusiastic, eager people, hungry to learn new tools for attracting a life partner. I tenderly called this bunch The Rowdy Group, as everyone in attendance was revved up and excited to release their BUT Blocks and attract a relationship. This was an unusually vocal gathering of spiritual people, which is one of my favorite kinds of interactive learning environments.

During this class, Ms. Hills (we'll call her Beverly), a mature lady dripping with emeralds and diamonds and wearing designer sportswear, spoke through her pinched lips and way-too-tight facelift while looking down the slope of her brand-new nose at the other attendees. Beverly fit the image the media paint of wealthy women living in the fabulous 90210 zip code. I liked Beverly instantly and was secretly hoping she would experience a profound breakthrough during our next three hours together.

Beverly, a somewhat nervous and shy person, sat right next to everyone's favorite personality, Patti. Patti was energetic and humorous. You will recall Patti as the *"I do want to fall madly in love again BUT, I'm afraid of getting hurt"* lady from earlier.

After discussing a series of examples of the pitfalls of having a Big BUT and how every one of us verbally or emotionally BUT ourselves dozens of time each day, Beverly glamorously raised her hand with movie star etiquette. "Eddie," she began, "I never use the word BUT while conversing with associates; therefore, I do not have a Big BUT!"

A potpourri of expressions flashed across people's faces as they considered Beverly's statement. Some rolled their eyes in disbelief, while others searched their brains to figure out if they themselves had ever used BUT in their vocabulary. A small handful of saucy personalities folded their arms in a playful gimme-a-break attitude.

Beverly sat next to Patti near the back of the room. Because of the room's layout and the structure of the chairs, Beverly did not see others rolling their eyes. Beverly's animated gestures caused her fingers to dance together like fairy wands ordained with precious emeralds, as if attempting to hypnotize us with the 90210 power of bling-bling.

Beverly resumed, "When my friends and I have the urge to use the word BUT in a sentence, we actually use a more sophisticated vernacular." Having everyone's attention, she proceed, "For example, we'll say the words 'however' or 'still' instead of the word BUT."

In that instant, she became entranced by her own rings and shimmering bracelets. I was excited that Beverly's offering was segueing into the next class segment of *BUT Stand-ins*. I asked her if she would mind sharing a couple of examples with our group. Beverly stated, "I have plenty of money; however, money can't buy me happiness."

She managed a faint smile while realizing for the first time what she was saying aloud. She attempted another approach, "I have everything I ever wanted, still I feel something is missing from my life."

Without skipping a beat, Patti turned in her chair to face Beverly and asked her, "Would that something you are missing just happen to be a man to share your life with?"

Everyone sensed the emotional brakes screeching to an abrupt halt in Beverly's gut. Beverly inhaled a deep, slow breath while addressing Patti, "I am open to having a relationship, if that's what you're asking?"

"It is!" Patti replied warmly, aware her question had evoked a level of vulnerability Beverly was uncomfortable expressing in public. Sensing that vulnerability, Patti instinctively reached over and gently touched Beverly's elbow, her eyes warm with genuine affection for her classmate's private sadness.

"Me too," Patti offered. "I'm looking for love, too," she added, taking the extra moment to really see Beverly's contradicted desire and Big BUT without judgment.

Mike, a burly, 250-pound quarterback riddled with testosterone, sat quietly in the middle of the class in a sea of women. Upon observing the interaction from beginning to end, he announced in his booming, baritone voice, "Hell, I'm looking for love, too!"

After a millisecond of delayed response, the entire group exploded with laughter and sincere smiles. Within seconds, all were basking in one wave of enlightenment after the other.

I appreciated Beverly's efforts to detach from her Big BUT with BUT Stand-Ins, *BUT* there was still a solid contradiction woven in the emotional fabric of her sentences and her desires.

The words BUT, *However, Still, Yet, Nevertheless,* and *Instead* vibrate the same and function the same, regardless of how we use them. To demonstrate this case in point, I wrote the following sentences on the board for our group while replacing the word BUT with *Big BUT Stand-ins*:

> I crave love; HOWEVER, I don't want to get hurt.
>
> I crave love; STILL, I don't want to get hurt.
>
> I crave love; YET, I don't want to get hurt.
>
> I crave love; NEVERTHELESS, I don't want to get hurt.

I crave love INSTEAD of hurt.

Our group agreed the *Stand-Ins* looked and sounded different than the word BUT, and in true energetic form, each *BUT Stand-in* basically felt the same in our gut. Ultimately, the Big BUT is the star and headlining act when it comes to contradicted desire in our lives. Whichever word we choose, whether it's the big cheese or a temporary stand-in, each word functions in complete association with the headliner. Stars and stand-ins alike oppose our desire, cancel our desire, or erase our desire all together, leaving the power of our old BUT belief standing in the spotlight alone.

Over the years, I have learned it is NOT the word that creates; it is how we vibrate while using the word that causes the creation. The higher the word's vibration takes us, the greater our physical results will be.

9

Riding the AND Avalanche

While facilitating Big BUT Workshops around the country, I ask attendees to finish the following sentence: "I really do want a relationship, BUT . . ." My pattern with this exercise is to ask the question with machinegun repetition and point to a new person each time I repeat it. The objective is to assist people in becoming familiar with their desires instead of their contradicted desires. The following is a list of answers to the infamous question, "I really do want a relationship BUT . . ."

> "BUT I don't want another jerk."
> "BUT not if they don't have a decent job."
> "BUT I don't want to get hurt."
> "BUT I don't want history to repeat itself."
> "BUT I don't want to waste my time."
> "BUT I'm afraid to commit to one person."
> "BUT I don't want to pay another man's bills."
> "BUT I don't have time to baby sit."
> "BUT I would rather be happy and single than in a relationship and miserable."

It was interesting to hear everyone's innate response to the question and fascinating to witness the similarities among the group. Though every response was different, you will notice each has a low-frequency feeling that contradicted each persons desire for love.

Mass conscious belief is an extraordinary phenomenon. It is also hard to buck when we are not feeling completely on our game. Meaning, when we feel low-frequency emotions for a long period of time about subject matter important to us, we will attract people, places, circumstances, and situations that promote and solidify our worse suspicions. In this case, the suspected belief is that love hurts.

The same is true, of course, of our best suspicions. Isn't it interesting to be in a human body while having complete access to the knowledge and wisdom of the Universe's heart and soul? More interesting still is that we often forget this gift is available to us. I believe the greater collective consciousness holds that on a core level, everything is operating like a well-oiled machine in perfect synchronicity with our higher, spiritual desire.

Our eager group conversed about our emotional discoveries around the "I really do want a relationship BUT" exercise, then together, we began a new approach.

With the next exercise, the stipulation was that their answers had to focus on their *DO WANTs* instead of their *DO NOT WANTs*. Sounds simple, right?

I asked a new person the exact same question three times in a row, hoping to find someone who could answer it without hesitation or contradiction. It is fun to ask this question in rapid-fire succession, one right after the other. You can literally see and feel each person called upon searching in the deepest archives of their subconscious mind while frantically reaching for a DO WANT answer.

The following answers are honest and true accounts from real people. Again, the new question was: "I really do want a relationship AND . . ."

> "AND . . . ugh . . . umm . . . I dunno?"
> "AND I don't want to get hurt as badly as before."
> "AND you're joking right?"
> "AND uh, what she said."
> "AND oh my goodness, I'm clueless."
> "AND I do want a relationship."
> "AND . . . this is a trick question isn't it?"
> "AND I want it to feel good. Can I ask for that?"

Their eyes grew to the size of saucers–flying saucers. Pauses, hesitation, and nervous energy complete with hand and arm movement abounded in our group. When I first began teaching Big BUT 101, I was surprised how hard it was for most people to openly discuss their much-deserved desires.

I have spent as much as 15 to 30 minutes on this exercise during workshops alone, as much time as it takes until one brave person takes a leap of faith from their existing programming and blurts three answers to the question aloud.

This example shows how our outdated responses are ingrained systems of thought that rattle to the forefront of our conscious mind, causing our mouths to automatically spew low-frequency data that negate our heartfelt desires. It is a habit to observe the low-frequency attributes around us. The real world–what we can easily see, touch, taste, hear, and smell–is considered a healthy approach. What about all the invisible frequencies that attracted our current circumstances and physical manifestations to us?

I believe we must look at our human soul personality as the multidimensional energy it is and take a new action that is purely inspired with the intention of our Intuitive Intellect or Universal Mind to back us up. Because most people had difficulty asking aloud for their desires, I created the **AND** *Avalanche* or, *AND-valanching.*

AND *Avalanches* are bridging tools that wean people from Big BUT Dis-ease and put them one thought and feeling at a time into their desires with little or no opposing belief to those desires. AND Avalanches promote one AND after the next, after the next, and after the next in fast repetition until we get used to *thinking* our desires in a format. The AND Avalanche is designed to replace the rickety old BUT shanty of our former beliefs and replace it with a new, solid foundation that supports our current dreams, goals, and aspirations.

How many AND Avalanches can you come up with? Create a list here for the desires you want to manifest in the area of love-life, financial freedom, or career. Take 60 seconds for this while coming up with as many AND Avalanches as you can. Good luck.

List your desired subject with AND Avalanches here:

1-

2-

3-

4-

5-

6-

7-

8-

9-

10-

The following is an example of an AND Avalanche. Once the group gets going on a positive free-for-all, there is no stopping the stampeding positive emotion pouring forth. We had a ton of fun creating this list, and I have confidence you will enjoy it as well. ***AND-valanches away!***

I desire a wonderful marriage
      AND I want it to be with my life mate
      AND I know it will feel easy and fluid
      AND I can feel it will be a win-win partnership
      AND I really want to laugh my Big BUT off with it
      AND I know it will be sexy, sensual, and delicious
      AND I want to appreciate, adore, and love him/her
      AND I want to appreciate, adore, and love myself
      AND I want it to have an element of pleasant surprises
      AND I want to focus on his/her positive attributes
      AND I want us to be the best we can be
      AND I want us to live this essence in the OVAL Mirror of life!

Using *AND* Avalanche Alternatives

And	With	That	Plus
Along with	Together with	As well as	
Also	In addition to	Including	

Using the SOUL-ution consciousness of the AND Avalanche Alternatives, your itty bitty, teeny weenie BUT can finally take its much-needed vacation back to the dictionary of tropical getaways so your Avalanche Alternatives can shine on the sturdy stage of your new desires. Joyously give these Alternatives the spotlight and center stage of your consciousness, allowing them to bask in one standing ovation vibration after another. Allow the lovely audience of your desires the glorious pleasure of appreciating you. Give this desire and belief permission to join in soul harmony and shout more, more, and more as the Universe answers one desire after the next.

Yippee!

On that note, bring your dreams, goals, and aspirations into the spotlight as they embrace the AND Alternatives. Open your mind and feelings for an energy-focusing game.

Please complete the following sentences while utilizing AND Alternatives to escalate the momentum of your wishes. Enjoy yourself, and truly have fun stretching from your old, past-tense, low-frequency beliefs into vibrating in your new, present-moment attitudes.

"I clearly wish for an amazing relationship"
WITH_____
AND_____
THAT_____

Focusing on the subject of money, let's repeat the exercise.

"I desire a lifestyle promoting consistent financial freedom"
ALONG WITH _____
TOGETHER WITH _____
AS WELL AS _____

Lastly, we focus attention on career or life purpose.

"I want a new career in which I am paid big bucks for being myself . . ."
ALSO _____
IN ADDITION TO _____
INCLUDING _____
PLUS _____

It feels good to know you are in the process of bringing outdated thought patterns to the forefront and replenishing your conscious and subconscious mind with **Vibratory Vocabulary**® that supports you. As we practice these techniques frequently throughout the day in our mind, speech, thoughts, journals, writing, self-relationships, actions, and feelings, our physical lives will begin to reflect our invisible attitudes into physical creations.

In November 2002, David Ault introduced me to John Livesay. John is the West Coast Director for *W* magazine. At the time, David was in the homestretch of his first book, *Where Regret Cannot Find Me*, which piqued John's enthusiasm to move forward with his own writing. John wanted to create a book to demonstrate his successful selling secrets with passion and integrity.

John took what my friend and Coach Melissa McFarland calls "Inspired Action" to produce his book. He set out to complete his writing in a relatively short amount of time, given his fulltime responsibility at *W*. He had a vision and strong desire, and he worked hard. John walked the talk his book would illustrate, thus turning his idea into an amazing reality.

In January 2004, David invited me to John's book launch party in Bel Air. I knew this was an unprecedented opportunity to practice the power of the **AND Avalanche** and the **TAGS Technique,** so off we went.

We arrived excited. The valet took David's car, then escorted us to a shuttle that climbed the half-mile driveway to a private home that was to die for. Celebrities maneuvered the red carpet and bright lights as dozens of paparazzi snapped pictures with the man of the hour and some of his famous guests.

John greeted us with warm hugs and led us to the red carpet to have our pictures taken with him. His eyes twinkled with excitement as handlers guided him from one important element of the party to the next.

Once inside the stately home it was abundantly clear that these folks were living in some serious high cotton.

Appreciative guests were surrounded by live music, jaw-dropping art, stunning esthetics, gorgeous design, fabulous fountains, brilliant swimming pools, decadent food and beverage, a perfect moonlit night, breathtaking views of the Los Angeles skyline, and a atmosphere abundant with grateful people celebrating one man's success. It was effortless to love the guests, AND the essence of the gathering, AND teenagers playing classical music, AND the cake. I can't believe I forgot the cake!

From the beginning of the evening to the very end, every aspect of John's function ran like universal clockwork. It was fun *TAGGING* beautiful things and interesting people, and observing John's happiness.

While maneuvering through the party, I had the realization that each of us gathered was a co-creator in John's intention. I couldn't help but realize that John must have had numerous visualizations about this event long before it occurred. This led me to recognize something important: that our big dreams do not have Big BUTS. We do. Our Soul or Higher Self never has contradicted energy. We do.

As physical consciousness, we are more invisible than we were taught to believe. Belief itself is an invisible reality. We must first hold the essential electricity of the invisible belief inside us purely before we can physically produce the basis of the belief. We were trained out of our nonphysical attributes and trained to be seers of the material world.

In that instant, I had greater appreciation for the power of visualization with pure desire. I adore creative personality types and more than that, I love to see what they manifest for themselves. I enjoy conversing with creative people about their creation techniques, their envisioned goals, and how they will produce their burning desires. It's inspiring to be around people that have moved from once having a poverty mindset and into prosperity consciousness.

John created a masterpiece based on his invisible desire and strong belief to create his first book, *The 7 Most Powerful Selling Secrets: Soar Your Way to Success with Integrity, Passion and Joy.* Even the title is imbued with energy.

Use AND-valanches every opportunity you have. Doing so raises your vibratory output, uplifts your emotional frequency, and magnetizes your good toward you even faster. Not to mention the fact that it centers you deeper into the heart of Appreciation.

10

Super Hero Punctuation Shields – BUT Armor

To write down our invisible thoughts, ideas, or emotions is an extraordinary way to pull our nonphysical attributes into physical manifestation. It is also a fun NEW way to break the Past Tense belief patterns that no longer serve us today in our Present Moment experience.

This is a great exercise to play with. It is also a predominately left-brain focused tool that feels good creatively.

The fastest way to stop a rampant BUT dead in its tracks is by the use any of the following devices. You guessed it, never underestimate the power of punctuation.

Any person can become a kick BUT superhero with the following ammunition. Okay, put away those Wonder Woman bulletproof bracelets and Xena breastplates, and get ready to replace them with the Big BUT Punctuation Shields. Get ready, set, and fire the ever-popular and highly underestimated Period, Exclamation Mark, and Comma. The words AND, WITH, and THAT provide additional ammunition.

This turns our once-contradicted desire into a clearly focused vibratory intention. Once again, our amazing class read aloud each sentence using their new BUT Armor. With each sentence, we held our hands softly over our solar plexus "stomach area" so our class could feel the difference in the vibration of the vocabulary and punctuation. Reading aloud as a group, the enthusiasm grew and the energy radiated higher. By the time we read the last sentence, the entire gathering felt uplifted about their new, non-contradicted declarations; even Beverly, Hills that is.

I desire love.   I desire love!
I desire love, happiness, *and* joy.
I desire love AND happiness!
I desire love WITH a win-win partner.
I desire love THAT amplifies my strengths and attributes.

It was good to see and experience everyone coming to life with a soulful articulation of their desires. This practice begins eliminating the Past Tense "Old Historical Patterns" of thinking and believing and begins to RE-build toward our desired reality. Practicing this technique over time puts a new concrete foundation in place NOW, today, so that when we do step into our future, our new foundation of desire is strong, sturdy, consistent, and REAL-istic.

We can believe we can have love that is uplifting and a bank account filled with money and the freedom it brings. It starts with a single, pure thought that carries a vibration.

Each NEW in the NOW thought vibrates our outdated BUT Beliefs deeper into the hibernating caves to sleep in the winter of our historical programming. Meanwhile, our new Present Moment Personality is building a solid foundation into the structure of our new life filled with an abundance of love, money, career, and much more.

Congratulations in advance for appreciating yourself and building bridges to your New in the NOW Empire of Desire.

Section Two:
The SOUL*ution*

11

Ten BUT BLASTERS –
Soul Tools to Fix Your BIG BUT

BUT Blasters are hi-frequency solutions that minimize our Big BUTS. When we flip the word solution into a hi-frequency Vibratory Vocabulary®, we get ***SOUL**ution*. Our Soul is a pure, nonphysical expression of the unconditional love that guides and supports us in life.

Making a conscious choice to focus on one or more of these hi-frequency tools can vaporize your big ass BUT into kingdom come.

Before you realize it, your old manner of observing the world will gradually melt away a little at a time, and all of a sudden, your new perspective becomes the familiar norm. Each moment you feel genuine good pouring through your mind, heart, and emotions, you are light years closer to living your full human-soul purpose.

Adults not only have Big BUTS, we focus on our BUTS more than necessary, whereas our Spirit, Soul, and Higher Self doesn't have a Big BUT at all. (Good Lord, can you imagine for just a second what the world would be like today if God-Universe had a Big BUT!?) "I'd like to let you into my pearly gates, Donald Trump, *BUT* you're fired!" Our invisible attributes are pure Universal Energy conspiring to bring our desires to us with great ease. The moment we consistently choose to observe thoughts and feelings that are But Free, we will begin living our personal heaven on earth.

The more time we spend in our personal BUT Blaster areas, the faster we can attract our desires and dreams coming true. I believe our dreams and visualizations are a thousand-fold stronger a reality than the physical world we live in. The only difference between our invisible world and our physical world is that we usually spend 90% more time in our physical world (what we can see and hear) while we spend less than 10% of our time and energy holding the pure vision and desire of what we do want in our lives.

Now I'm no mathematical genius, BUT even I can see the scale hugely tipped 90% more in the direction of what is not wanted in this scenario. As a result of this daily dilemma in our lives, I've decided it would be hi-frequency fun to share Ten BUT Blasters for you to experiment with.

As promised, here are Ten Spiritual *SOUL*-utions promoting and empowering us to focus on our desire without contradicting that desire with a Big BUT Belief:

1- The TAGS Technique®
2- Feeling Good
3- Laughter and Humor
4- Nature
5- Music and Harmonics

6- Praying with a Pure Heart
7- Vibratory Vocabulary®
8- Artistic Expression
9- Visualization and Imagination
10- Day Dreams and Night Dreams

BUT Blaster One   The TAGS Technique

"If only the people who worry about their liabilities would think about the riches they do possess, they would stop worrying. Would you sell both your eyes for a million dollars . . . or your legs . . . or your hands . . . or your hearing? Add up what you do have, and you'll find that you won't sell them for all the gold in the world. The best things in life are yours, if you can appreciate yourself."

- Dale Carnegie

The TAGS Technique is the easiest and purest form of merging with Universal Consciousness. When we appreciate, we light up like a million stars on a clear night. Appreciation is a clear, laser-like signal of adoration and unconditional love from us to the Universe and back again, creating a full circle of pure desire with pure manifestation of that desire.

Appreciation is a living energy that activates our inner light and our soul knowing. This light and knowing penetrate all time and space reality, as we physically know it to be, and surpasses all worlds to get our signal of appreciation to the powers that be. Thus, appreciation is the most effortless and effective manner in which to communicate with the Universe in a consistent manner so that we may reap heavenly results here on Earth.

It was through utilizing the power of Appreciation that I created a playful tool I call the **TAGS Technique**®. The TAGS Technique employs the principles of:

Thanksgiving
Appreciation
Gratitude and
Sending **S**oul **S**ignals

And presto, we have **TAGS**®!

Although Thanksgiving, Appreciation, and Gratitude basically mean the same thing, they each feel a touch different from the other. My clients seem to respond to Appreciation and Gratitude over the feeling of Thanksgiving. Or, as my friend Marissa says with noted humor, "Thanksgiving reminds me of food, and food makes me hungry." She's a good little eater. Everyone's different. It is our different beliefs and different desires that make the world an extraordinary place to live.

I can honestly say it is easy to find something every hour that I am thankful for, that I appreciate, or that makes me feel happy that I am able to continue doing what I love to do for a living.

The power of our feelings is barely seen as a viable catalyst in creating our human reality. I predict you will continue to see a trend in the next ten to twenty years of authors writing and speaking on nothing but the power of our human feelings and emotions. It will be especially exciting when the scientific and medical communities come together and consistently acknowledge that our hi-frequency emotions and low-frequency emotions create our physical lives. While today the power of feelings still seems unimportant, in the coming years it will be seen as leading-edge thought.

Consciously using the power of Thanksgiving, Appreciation, and Gratitude activates and sends pure, laser-focused *Soul Signals* into the heart and soul of the Universe. The Soul Signals we send to the Universe through the art of the TAGS Technique is just a smidgeon of how we can consciously co-create with our Soul Electricity:

Our Focus + Our Feelings = Our Reality

Our Soul Self is working for us unconditionally, even when we forget to take good care of ourselves. When we forget to look at, think about, or focus on the things in our lives that enhance our personal experience, our Soul Electricity holds a vigil of unconditional love and eternal support.

As the power of our **Soul Electricity**® becomes global knowledge, people will be less likely to contradict their desires and beliefs about love, money, and career and instead will feel empowered to deliberately create miracles in those areas of their lives.

BUT Blaster Two **Feeling Good**

"First feelings are always the most natural."

- Louis XIV

Feeling Good sounds like more metaphysical woo-woo that's much to do about nothing, but don't cross this petite morsel of life-changing material out of your little black book of conscious co-creating the life you want just yet. I have understood the meat and potatoes of feeling good since the age of seven or eight, and I remember it today as if it were yesterday.

The season was fall, my favorite in the Carolinas. Cool sunlight broke through the trees, its light amplifying millions of brightly colored leaves that clung to their homes among the trees surrounding our property. Each caressing breeze animated these treasures of beauty everywhere I looked. The early foliage of ruby reds, amber golds, and cinnamon orange showered past me, escorted by the sound of rustling tree limbs in the afternoon sky as I sat on an oil drum watching my mom hang our family's laundry on the clothesline behind our home.

Mom didn't know I was perched quietly on the 50-gallon drum, mesmerized by the crisp, fresh air and the sound of her singing and humming songs under her breath while she worked. The feeling of peace and goodness in the air that afternoon was transforming and abundant. We didn't have much in the way of physical wealth, but on this afternoon, I was the richest kid in the state.

Mom was always a serious and responsible person who rarely took a break from work or life. She often moved from one household chore or yard project to the next, tired and exhausted to the bone from long shifts in a textile mill, family errands, and our school activities. The hours never stopped her from preparing home-cooked meals, keeping a spotless home, and tending a well-manicured lawn.

Her attention and love were never focused on herself, but on her four boys. Because she was so intent on getting things done with hardly time to breathe between chores and work, it surprised me to hear her singing. When she wasn't singing, she was humming with a pleasant, relaxed expression on her face. I loved seeing my mom in such a feel-good, radiant space.

This day felt like a blessing for everyone it touched. My senses were on pleasant overload watching mom in the amber-golden light, singing softly as she did her chores--chores I realized for the first time were designed to make her kids' lives better and enhance her own life as a good mother.

The moment became fairy-tale like. For an instant, I sensed I was someplace greater than my private oil-drum sanctuary. A surge of energy tickled my solar plexus, delivering a message that covered me with goose bumps. My eyes watered with the rich, hi-frequency message that came from the spirit of the afternoon.

"God Is Good," reverberated in unison through my mind, heart, and solar plexus in perfect sync.

It was not the words that convinced and converted me right there on the oil drum, but the shear emotional electricity I felt in every cell and molecule in my being. It was a combination of the day and its beauty, of observing my mom as she felt good and allowing myself to slip into the abundance of the moment and experience the complete richness of the afternoon.

Something bigger than the love I felt for Mom happened inside of me that day, something I have carried my whole life.

Every single moment we choose to feel good in life, we choose a higher awareness that harmonizes our invisible dreams, goals, and aspirations into a physical manifestation. When we feel good, and that *God is Good*, we activate our true essence, we create miracles, and we are more likely to live the life we were born to live.

Feeling good, feeling God (or Universe) is a sure BUT Blaster. I love finding new things to feel good about. Give yourself permission to go on a Feeling Good Free-for-all. Find anything and everything in your imagination and physical reality that makes you feel good, gooder, goodest, and GREAT! The longer you experience this hi-frequency goodness coming to you and pouring through you, the faster you successfully pull the goodness in life to you. Have fun and enjoy yourself.

BUT Blaster Three   Laughter and Humor

"Before my gratitude journal began, there were things out in the world that I wished never existed, like mosquitoes."

- Ellen Degeneres

Laughter is one of the most healing gifts we posses. There is a reason situation comedies abound on national television, comediennes like Ellen Degeneres have hugely successful shows, and Jim Carrey makes $20 million a movie to make people laugh. Comedy clubs, plays, movies, radio stations, books, magazines, children's games, and even traffic schools have chosen to add fun and amusing twists and turns to their formats. Why? Because they have discovered that when we are feeling good, we get more accomplished. Approaching important tasks from a hi-frequency perspective with tools like humor and laughter facilitates learning difficult tasks easily, increases productivity, and enhances our ability to live a longer, healthier life.

The other day, I heard a comedian on television say his only tool to survive growing up in the New York projects was to get the other kids to laugh at him or to laugh with him. This comic's belief was that if you could get the bullies to laugh with you, they would be less likely to beat the crap out of you.

Laughing is an unpolluted hi-frequency action that raises our vibration and can raise the vibration of others around us. It simply feels good to laugh and feels better when others laugh with us. Laughing erases color lines, prejudices, hurts, heartaches, negative emotions, and blame, to name a few.

Children laugh hundreds of times a day, while adults only laugh an average of five to seventeen times a day. Access that natural comedian/comedienne inside you, the one called your soulful, inner child, and give that animated aspect of you permission to tickle your funny bone. Make a conscious feel-good decision to lock into the aspects of your life that cause you to smile and laugh.

Start with a smile first. Smile with yourself before you leave for work in the morning. Direct your winning smile toward your co-workers and give out genuine healing smiles to people you don't even know. Watch how contagious your smile feels and how a simple smile can raise your energetic vibration and then ripple out to the world.

After a few hours of sharing your smile, you will notice the caliber of person around you begins to change. Smiling often leads to pleasant exchanges of energy with others. Pleasant exchanges of energy lead to humor, and humor leads to laughter. Smiling, humor, and laughter will always create an enormous chain of synchronicity that enhances and enlightens our lives and the lives of others. Go ahead–smile!

Smile from the inside out. Think of something funny that lifts your thoughts to a lighthearted pitch. Can you remember a funny moment from the past that caused you to howl with laughter? A moment when you laughed so hard that the soda you were drinking flew out of your nose like an open fire hydrant valve on a hot summer day? Or a time you and your friends were laughing so hard that neither of you could catch your breath or say a word without starting a whole new avalanche of self-inflicted laughter again? Now that's laughing your Big BUT off!

Treat yourself and share a smile with someone you love and care about. What better person to share your genuine smile with than YOU!

BUT Blaster Four   Nature

"All nature wears one Universal grin."

- Henry Fielding

Nature is an entire world of perfection within itself that causes us to believe once and for all that there is something bigger and greater than our elementary human comprehension can grasp. Nature has a rhythm unto itself that humankind has attempted to tap into and duplicate since Adam and Eve.

The most effortless way to tap into nature's majesty is to be in it, appreciate it, and honor it. It is almost impossible to be in nature and not be filled with a sense of goodness and appreciation.

One of my favorite and most influential metaphysical teachers is Abraham-Hicks. Abraham is channeled by a lovely lady from Texas. Each Abraham-Hicks Publication tape comes with a question and answer segment asking simple questions about daily life. Abraham answers their questions strictly from a nonphysical perspective while shining clarity on the stage of our human experience.

It was on a Tape-of-the-Month that I heard Abraham say to the audience, "Have you ever seen a tree worried about paying a mortgage? Do you think the ocean wonders what its property value is these days?" Abraham went on to say that every aspect of nature is tuned in, tapped in, and turned on to the stream of pure, positive energy that creates worlds. When nature asks for something, it allows the Universe to deliver its request.

Trees do not justify their existence; the ocean does not justify its reason for being. Only humans justify and contradict their desires with resistance, aka The Big BUT Syndrome. We ask the Universe for what we say we want, then we justify why we should have it, why it should have already been here, and then we often blame some other person or thing in our lives as the cause for why we don't have it.

We could learn a lot from the power of nature. When animals ask, they allow. When a tree asks, the tree allows. When the ocean asks, the ocean allows its requested good to come to it. This happens not because the animals, trees, and ocean deserve to have it, but because they simply exist. Nature understands it is worthy and deserving to have what it asks for simply because it exists in perfect harmony with All That Is. When people learn to ask for what they desire without opposing their desires with resistance, they will easily attract the manifestation of their desires.

Nature seems to be the place we run to in an attempt to regain lost balance. Thoughts that have overwhelmed us and internal dialogues that weigh heavy on our hearts seem to melt away as clarity and decision arrive within the majesty of a great forest or on the shores of a brilliant beach rich with treasures, beauty, and connection to our Source.

Nature was a main source of solace for me even before I entered the first grade. Our family moved to the country, to a rural, two-acre spot that bordered cow pastures, sloping hills, and a meandering creek that skirted two sides of our new property.

When things in our household were hectic or overwhelming, I retreated to the thin veil of woods behind our home or to the meadows that nestled the woods and stretched for miles. I loved to lie in the grassy carpet of pasture and watch the sky stretch for all eternity, as my intuition and imagination delivered messages and images of wellness that were sure to come from the adversity and conflict our family was going through at the time. I would often sit on the banks of the creek in a glassy-eyed daze as the minnows, crawdads, snapping turtles, and bullfrogs danced beneath the water's murky surface.

Walking in the woods, sitting in the infamous five-limb tree, or lying in the meadow was my escape from the physical drama in my life and a retreat back to my whole soul-self.

Over time, my conflict and confusion about the whys of life subsided into brilliant balance and conscious clarity. My smile and love of life returned, and my happiness was restored with each abbreviated retreat to the pure, positive energy nature unconditionally provided me.

Desert landscapes and mountain ranges not only deliver us fresh clean air, but a delicious new perspective. It is in nature that we *can* see the forest for the trees and see the light at the end of the tunnel and essentially get out of our own way long enough to savor the hi-frequency healing all around us.

Nature restores and fills us with hi-frequency fuel that we take back to our homes and workplaces. It gifts us with the soul alignment, wholeness, and sense of well-being we lost somewhere during endless errands, carpooling, and frustrating careers in which we are overworked and underappreciated. As a matter of fact, I strongly believe nature saved my mom's life more than once.

As I said earlier, my mom worked nonstop for our family. Endless hours of working her fingers and her spirit to the bone did not slow her down, even when the doctors took half her left lung in 1973 due to a misdiagnosis of tuberculosis. Mom pulled herself back from the depths of a month-long hospital stay to take care of her young'uns. Before we knew it, Mom was back in full force and though she was in great pain, she rarely allowed us to see it.

Mom was on an automatic pilot of never-ending, 18-hour workdays. I rarely saw her sit still for any amount of time, except when our family vacationed at the beach. Mom's transformation from the daily chores and hard work of real life melted away with every breath of salt air she inhaled as we approached the North Carolina coast. The muscles in her face would soften, the tension in her neck and shoulders would subside, and the lovely twinkle in her eyes would return. As we neared the beach, she became more childlike, even giddy, with her eagerness and expectation of what the beach always provided her. And when we could actually see the ocean, her soul-self would return as she dissolved into a deep, peaceful trance of appreciation. Her sense of humor, contagious spirit, and full heart lavished each of us with verbal hugs, and her abundant smiles spoke nonverbal I love yous that were priceless.

The beach has always been Mom's favorite place to visit. It makes her feel healed, whole, and healthy again. It restores her spirit and renews her faith that everything will be okay.

In 1997-98 the doctors took the remaining half of Mom's left lung. She was in and out of the hospital between November and January, and almost died three times during her recovery period. It was a scary time for all of us. For a long time after her surgeries, things looked dismal. I have never prayed so much in my lifetime as I did during those four months. Then, the funniest thing happened. In the late spring of 1998, my Aunt Shirlee organized a two-week trip to Myrtle Beach and invited the family to come with her. Mom and I orchestrated our schedules to join my aunt for one week.

Mom still felt the severity of the surgeries for months. With only one lung, her breathing was difficult and more labored. The simplest things in life were huge obstacles to her now. Things like bending over to vacuum or walk the driveway for the daily mail made her life a living hell. As if that wasn't enough, she was having trouble battling the humidity of the

North Carolina summers. Just leaving the comfort of her air-conditioned home became an issue. Now, just the thought of going to the ocean soothed and transformed her spirit just as it had when we were children.

I flew in from California and joined Mom, and together we drove to the coast to meet up with Aunt Shirlee. We laughed and girl-talked during the five-hour commute and once again, as we neared the coastline, Mom could smell the salt air, and her metamorphosis quickly began.

We arrived in the early evening with a near full moon that lit the night sky. The moment Mom could hear and see the ocean, heaven was restored again in every cell of her being. In a sense, Mom was home. Her spirit was back in full force. I was relieved.

Early the next day, Mom and most of our extended family walked four miles on the beach. She was energized and happy again. Everyone was relieved to see her physically and emotionally gravitating back to her soul-self. I felt blessed, and I thanked God Universe for answering our prayers.

The attributes nature provides Mom and all of us are priceless. We simply need to remember to take advantage of its infinite possibilities.

When we are not physically out in nature, our Soul brings aspects of nature to us. Domestic pets, houseplants, flowers, water fountains, stones, trees, and materials for landscaping are simple expressions of our connection to the healing energies of the nature kingdom. It's no wonder home improvement centers and pet stores make a killing these days.

In the future, don't wait until you are sick and tired of the same old daily grind of life before you get away to the replenishing, revitalizing elements of nature. Make a heartfelt promise to get outside at least once a week. Getting back to nature can give you the clarity and alignment you deserve.

BUT Blaster Five   Music and Harmonics

"Music produces a kind of pleasure which human nature cannot do without."

- Confucius

Music is an authentic universal language that can completely stop any clock ever made. It transcends time and space reality with its tones, harmonics, and vocals, the whole time raising our vibration and often transporting us back to moments in our past that we had long forgotten.

In the fall of 2002, while riding with my friend Max, he popped a compilation CD into his car stereo. He had made the CD himself, burning all types of music from Broadway, Pop, and Rhythm and Blues, to the Oldies of the 60s and 70s. When the song "Downtown" came through the speakers of Max's car stereo, my mind and emotions immediately recaptured a forgotten moment from my youth. It was a time in my childhood when my mom listened to high-energy songs on her car radio while running errands with us kids.

I remembered the first time I heard "Downtown," as well as the time of year it was, the clothes I wore, and my mom's mood. I was in the front seat of the car, my bare feet inches from touching the floorboard as Petula Clark belted out the words to "Downtown" over Mom's car radio. Mom effortlessly glided her giant Bat Mobile of a Cadillac up and down the curving country roads. Around each bend and turn, I remembered my childhood body having no power over the laws of gravity as each twist in the snakelike road before me caused my body to float along the slick leather seats. I thought to myself, "I can't wait to be old enough for my feet to touch the floorboard."

I called to mind my mom sharing her Coca-Cola with me. Back in those days, she put a small pack of salted nuts in her bottled Coke, long before sodas were sold in aluminum cans. I felt the cool soda pop bottle on my lips and experienced, for the first time, the soda's sweet carbonated tickle commingled with the zest of salty peanuts.

Mom smiled when I made a contorted face as the taste sensations swirled around in my mouth, burning my nose and causing my eyes to water. It was one of those rare warm and fuzzy episodes in my youth when everything felt just perfect, and I am almost positive it wasn't the gas bubbles in my stomach that caused my euphoria.

In one hundredth of a second, a distant memory flooded my consciousness, superimposing itself over my current reality more than 30 years later. During this multidimensional experience, it was effortless to feel both realities overlapping each other, creating a dual experience. It was a wonderful experience that pleasantly reminded me of the power of our subconscious mind.

The synchronicity of one song managed to erase space and time, 2,600 miles, and 32 years to be exact. The same song I heard when I was ten years old reactivated the same high feelings inside me in the fall of 2002, causing two worlds to unite in a climax of emotion and memory.

In the passenger's side of Max's car, I appreciated the healing quality of music and how it affects and changes our lives. As we sailed through the ravines of Laurel Canyon Boulevard, singing the words to "Downtown," I felt like a kid again, with that same funny taste in my memory, feeling pleased that my big toes almost touched the floorboard of that old Bat Mobile.

Music has that ability. It activates and awakens emotions within us. When we hear a song for the first time that makes us feel good, chances are that if we don't hear that same song for another 32 years, we will still feel good when we hear it again, and we will awaken and remember what we were doing, thinking, and feeling the first time we heard it.

Thought and feeling create more of our experience than all action and words put together. Whether the music we're enjoying is with or without lyrics, it is always the vibration of the music and the intention behind it that raises our individual frequency from common to extraordinary.

Can you recall the Coca-Cola commercial from the 70s, "I'd like to teach the world to sing in perfect harmony; I'd like to buy the world a Coke . . ."? I loved that ad campaign. I adored the way it felt and was captivated by its simple visual and auditory message. People of all races, colors, and creeds stood side by side in unison, singing and deliberately vibrating the verbal and "invisible frequency" of peace and harmony among all peoples.

The exact moments I experienced that Coke commercial, I believed it was possible to create harmony on a global level. The music appropriated for a simple soft drink commercial actually brought desire and a pure belief for 30 seconds to the mass consciousness, causing us to hold the vision that all people can get along, if only for a few moments.

Music is a feeling medium that awakens our emotional attributes. These emotional attributes are extensions of our nonphysical energy, our Soul, if you will. As we marry the emotional aspects of our being to the physical aspects of our being, we can live a fulfilled experience. Music offers an escape from our limited habit of thinking and feeling and gives us permission to forget the worry, fear, and concerns so we can live a better quality of life.

Listen to music that lifts your heart and soul. Sing all your favorite songs that carry you to the high points of your past and to the unlimited potential of your future. Choose a new theme song for yourself every week or so, and use each new theme song as your cheerleader, reminding you to think outside your normal, everyday reality. Allow the spirit of the music to awaken your soulful attributes and fuel your nonphysical desires into amazing physical manifestations.

One afternoon while reviewing some material, I had the TV on for background noise and was only half listening to VH-1.

Suddenly, I heard the words to "It's the Real Thing" pouring out of the television set. Racing into the living room I saw my favorite commercial for Coca-Cola from the 70s displayed on the set with a commentary. It turns out my favorite commercial "musically speaking" is also the nation's favorite commercial as well. It was voted the number-one commercial of all time by VH-1.

BUT Blaster Six   **Praying with a Pure Heart**

"If the only prayer you say in your whole life is "Thank you," that would suffice."

- Meister Eckhart

Praying with a pure heart is simply praying with a rich emotional energy that feels like the outcome for which you are praying. If you are praying for happiness for yourself or for a loved one, you want to pray beyond physical words and action. You want to pray with the highest emotional frequency the cells and atoms in your physical body can muster.

Charles Haddon Spurgeon said, "Whether we like it or not, asking is the rule of the Kingdom." The purest form of asking is through prayer and authentic appreciation. Keep in mind that you are one with God Universe, that you are more nonphysical in your adult body than you are physical. We are born with the wisdom, knowledge, power, and love of the cosmos inside us. Our soul-self is infinite wisdom bringing our spiritual and human attributes together as one in order to fulfill our emotional frequencies.

The most powerful prayers we send are the ones launched from a platform of feeling excited, happy, uplifted and connected to our whole soul-self. The higher we raise our invisible frequencies inside our physical bodies, the faster our prayers are answered.

Another secret of praying purely is to talk about, observe, and vibrate the solution, or ***SOUL***-ution, of our desires. We may want to change our old prayer habits to include lighthearted tools that speak to our unique belief systems.

As a child, I was raised to pray from a serious adult perspective. This approach took a lot of the animated electricity and plain ole fun out of praying.

In today's world, there are myriad ways to express our energy through the art of praying. We sing our prayers. We light candles and listen to music that matches the spirit of our prayers. We walk out in nature and appreciate the world around us. We follow alternative avenues of healing and new thought processes that revolutionize the old way of doing things, bringing these new perceptions into our old method of prayer.

Because I believe God has a great sense of humor, I firmly believe laughter, humor, and living life with a light heart and a fun-loving soul is a must-do action that facilitates our prayers being answered in record speed.

Music, prayer, chanting, affirmations, and just plain feeling good are powerful healing modalities. When we merge these powers together as ONE, every cell, atom, and molecule in our bodies resonates with its pure frequency.

Praying and chanting with music as a catalyst is an absolute Energetic Multiple Orgasmic Combustion Point. Karen Drucker's music has masterfully perfected this art form. Her

Songs of the Spirit I, Songs of the Spirit II, and *Beloved* albums illustrate this example perfectly.

Karen's music is a permanent fixture in my home and heart. Her music is a series of brilliant vocals, chants, and songffirmations that marry our loving spirit and human selves together as one.

BUT Blaster Seven   Vibratory Vocabulary

"One forgets words and one forgets names. One's vocabulary needs constant fertilization or it will die."

- Evelyn Waugh

Every word in every language radiates an invisible vibratory frequency. Even our names and birthdates, when spoken aloud, register energetic vibration. For example, many psychics will often ask you to write or speak your full birth name or date of birth in order to receive an electromagnetic impulse. It is the invisible vibration of our vocabulary that carries energy inside it. Healers and energy interpreters can sense, feel, and know things based on these vibrations.

Everyone knows what vocabulary is, BUT few people realize the words they are using could be the very thing that stops their desired good from coming to them. For example, how many times have you used the word "money" in your thoughts and words?

More often than not, the word "money" has a low, lethargic vibration that surrounds it. It is not using the word that brings us the money, it is how we ultimately feel about the green stuff that determines whether we can consistently magnetize it to us or not.

Bernice Kanner, author of *Are You Normal About Money,* says "One in five Americans confessed that they often worry about money. Fifty-five percent think about it only when they're managing it, and 23 percent let their minds drift to it occasionally."

How do you FEEL when you think about the subject of money? Can you feel prosperous while observing it in your mind's eye?

Or a better question is, when you get your paycheck at the end of a long, hard workweek, do you feel it is a fair exchange of money to compensate you for all your hard work? Or do you feel it is not an appropriate match to the number of hours you've put in?

If you answered that you don't feel the monetary compensation is fair for the number of hours you worked, you are vibrating a low frequency about the word money. Or, better stated: If you are saying affirmations to attract more money to yourself, there is a great chance you are radiating a low-frequency vibration each and every time you think the word money, say the word money, and take action toward making more money. This is the ultimate big BUT in that you are saying and doing all of the right things, BUT you are vibrating a low-frequency vibration that is literally keeping your money at bay, regardless of how hard you work to obtain more of the green stuff.

Each of us desires money for different reasons. I would say the primary reason for wanting more money is because we believe it will bring us one or more of the following:

Comfort	Security	Flexibility	Assurance
Freedom	Ease	Release	Sanctuary
Spontaneity	Independence	Relief	Solace

In the space below, write the word "money" five times in a row.

Does the feeling of this word vibrate a high, pure frequency? Or, does it vibrate a low, heavy frequency? If you felt a heaviness in your Solar Plexus Megaphone®, you are asking for the money you want and feeling the lack of money at the same time.

Now, pick one of the words listed below that you feel has a high, pure frequency. Write it five times slowly, paying attention to how it vibrates in your body while writing it.

Comfort	Security	Flexibility	Assurance
Freedom	Ease	Release	Sanctuary
Spontaneity	Independence	Relief	Solace

Again, does the feeling of your new vibratory vocabulary feel like a high, pure frequency, or a low, heavy frequency?

Make a conscious choice to use all the vocabulary you can that radiates a high vibration. The higher the vibration, the faster your desires come to you. The sooner you use the art of vibratory vocabulary, the sooner you eliminate the Big BUT Syndrome from your life. Happy vibrating!

BUT Blaster Eight   Artistic Expression

"Each of us makes his own weather, determines the color of the skies in the emotional universe which he inhabits."

- Fulton J. Sheen

I have heard it said that the Universe is the ultimate artist, the greatest creator, and each of is a co-creator with All That Is. I believe this.

Artistic creativity originates in the nonphysical world. This creative force then races toward the Earth plane, pouring to and through anyone who is an open channel to receive its unconditional gifts.

We ourselves are actual God Art originating in the nonphysical realm. With a combination of our freewill to choose and our parents' intention to give birth to us, we moved our unlimited consciousness to Earth, where we blended our God Self into a physical personality.

From our nonphysical point of view, we clearly understand that our essential energy creates our physical experience. Our soul instincts remind us that our every thought and feeling entertains and influences the world around us. The same thoughts and feelings that designed and sculpted our invisible realities then are, in this exact moment, sculpting our life today.

Feeling creative or expressing art from a creative platform generates an amazing vortex of timeless energy that encompasses our physical personality. In comparison, our human shell is merely a grain of sand in the grand scheme, and our soul is actually God Universe. In essence, our body and soul are one and the same, not separate. This means we have unlimited co-creative power to sculpt both our physical reality and nonphysical reality alike.

We are a masterpiece imagined from the heart and soul of the ultimate artist, God Universe. Just as Michelangelo created the sculpture David or Leonardo De Vinci painted the Mona Lisa, God Universe created the ultimate living art, us! It is my strong belief that over time, the art and artist are designed and created to become one.

Recently, I met RJ and Nick, both professional dancers and both artists who used their Soul Electricity to paint on the physical canvas of their lives. RJ and Nick have danced with icons in the music and movie industry. For most people, what would be a once-in-a-lifetime opportunity to meet their favorite stars is a lifestyle for RJ and Nick.

I asked RJ when he consciously knew in his heart he was destined to dance professionally. He replied that he had always known. He recalled knowing at the tender age of three that he wanted to dance. RJ booked his first audition off a dance scholarship he won as teenager and shortly after, he was dancing on tour with Cher.

I also asked him how it felt to dance on stage in front of fifty thousand screaming fans. RJ recollected, "The moment I stepped from behind the curtain and onto the stage, the wind was knocked out of me. It was like an out-of-body experience."

Nick described how artists like Madonna, Janet Jackson, and others inspired him. As a child, Nick felt a strong connection to their music, dance, and creative expression. I asked Nick when he realized he wanted to be a professional dancer. "I gravitated to material like Janet Jackson's *Rhythm Nation* and Madonna's *Truth or Dare* movie." These documentaries, with their behind-the-scenes footage of the dancers, props, and artistic direction, grabbed Nick's imagination and burning desire. In these moments, Nick felt the world he observed and appreciated on the TV screen would someday be the world in which he would dance.

Nick has completed a tour with Britney Spears and is now touring with Janet Jackson. Today, Nick and RJ can be seen on the big and small screens living out their childhood dreams.

It is true everything around us is a genuinely felt, creative expression. Pure art is genius. John Hersey said, "True genius rearranges old material in a way never seen before." By definition, a person who performs his or her work as if it were art, is an artist.

From a mansion in the Hollywood Hills to a cardboard box housing the homeless, we design our reality with the power of free will, observation, and choice. When I was a kid, I overheard my mom tell my aunt, "Eddie is good at making chicken salad out of chicken sh--." I didn't know exactly what she meant at the time. I do know that it felt good to me when I heard it.

We all have the ability to take nothing and turn it into a masterpiece. Or better stated, even if we are living in a poverty environment, we absolutely have the ability to take our soul attributes of pretending, imagining, daydreaming, and fantasizing and turn how we perceive our poverty environment into something that feels and vibrates a feel-good, prosperity consciousness.

We have the free will to observe what we choose to observe. What we choose to observe causes us to feel either high or low pulsations of emotional energy. God Universe then responds to these pulsations by bringing us the physical manifestation caused by our invisible pulsations.

Every pulsation we emanate is a creation, an expression of our soul and human personality. Every pulsation we generate enhances either our prosperity or our poverty consciousness (or low-frequency attributes).

As an artist observing negativity, we will create more negativity on the canvas of our life. Likewise, a soul artist observing beauty creates a life filled with beautiful, artful experiences.

An artist who utilizes his or her soul electricity consistently in daily life would look something like this: You are an artist with unlimited potential. You love harnessing inspirational ideas and creative solutions. You are revered for donating your time, energy, and creativity to the masses while making the world a better place to live through your generous accomplishments. In a few short years you, your art, and your humanitarian contributions are synonymous with global achievement and genuine greatness.

Everything you touch turns to gold. You take complete responsibility for creating your life through your feelings and emotions. You are loved, and you have captured the richest meaning of self-love and self-esteem. You appreciate the extravagant lifestyle you have produced while doing what you enjoy. You have great friends, a lovely partner, a beautiful home, and financial freedom. You are living your purpose and fulfilling your destiny. You are on top of the world.

Meanwhile, a low-frequency artist may look something like this: You are painting on the canvas of life with your mundane thoughts and numbed feelings. You dip your brush into the endless colors of thought available, and the instant your paintbrush touches your canvas, the brilliant paint colors immediately fade into lifeless, mustard yellow. Frustrated, you reach for a cold lump of clay to mold and sculpt it into a beautiful relationship. The clay is bulky, resistant, and doesn't do what you want it to do in order to make you happy. You blame the clay for not turning out the way you wanted it to. The clay fades to a mustard yellow hue of nothingness.

Desperate to express your creative essence, you decide on one last-ditch attempt to create happiness. Irritated, you decided you'll write poetry, music, or a bestselling book that uplifts people. The poetry is harder than you thought. The music feels good, BUT there are more starving musicians than rich ones. The book isn't writing itself as you'd planned. At this point, the poetry, music, and book also disappear into the same raggedy, everyday yellow that refuses to allow you the freedom of expressing your invisible desire on the physical canvas of life.

Finally, you give up. The authority figures were right. You can't get by in life just dreaming and imagining on the creative and artistic side of life. After all, it's not realistic, and it is certainly not making you a responsible, play-by-the-rules citizen. So, you give up and seek out that safe, dependable, 9-to-5 job and let go of your soul artistry.

We've all had the experience of taking the brilliant colors life offers and painting a reality with those colors only to see that our end result is bland yellow instead of the vibrant masterpiece we began. Art, like all things, takes practice, patience, and a playful approach. The first time our paintbrush touches the canvas, it usually doesn't represent what we see in our imagination. In fact, it often looks kind of scary.

We are here to explore the animation of our imagination, to perform new techniques in our thoughts and physically place both on this canvas called the human experience. Over time, with playful practice strokes, the colors of our imagination become fine-tuned, realistically aligned, and physically beautiful. Our pretend dreams become a physical reality, for what we imagine in our minds and feelings eventually becomes what we live and breathe.

This is life.

Which artist do you identify with most, the first artist on top of the world or the frustrated artist experiencing life through the complacent monotone lens?

As an artist who creates life, what is your free will, choice, and observation locked onto?

Are you observing the art of physical poverty or observing the art of pleasant prosperity?

BUT Blaster Nine   Visualization and Imagination

"Just because a man lacks the use of his eyes doesn't mean he lacks vision."

- Stevie Wonder

You cannot talk about the art of visualizing without thinking about Shakti Gawain and her monumental accomplishments with the books *Creative Visualization* and *The Creative Visualization Workbook - Use the Power of Your Imagination to Create What You Want in Your Life*. I have always believed imagination and focused feelings create our lives. Shakti set a superb standard in her books by showing us how to redirect our innate power of imagination in a step-by-step manner in order to create the life we want.

The first time I used Shakti's *Creative Visualization Workbook*, I was waiting for my business partner to finish her meeting with a psychic. I sat outside in a park by the psychic's apartment, lost in my workbook for almost two hours. I wrote lists, created goals, and drew pictures about specific areas in which I wanted to create success. I was drawing a picture of the house I would buy my Mom, when my business partner called me into the office for my intuitive reading. I had been working on this page for almost 20 minutes, doodling little details about Mom's future property and really allowing my imagination to flow in a natural way. I closed my book and stored it in my backpack, zipped it up, and quickly went inside for my time slot. I had not sat with the psychic more than 60 seconds when she looked at me and said, "I don't know what you're worried about young man. You're going to buy your mother a house one day."

My mouth dropped open and my jaw hit the floor. Neither my partner nor the psychic saw or knew what I was doing outside while they were together.

In that exact moment, I realized the power of visualization and imagination. I felt great drawing and imagining with Shakti's books. I loved using the power of my Intuitive Intellect to create Mom's house in my thoughts, feelings, and imagination, then writing and drawing what I saw in my head onto the paper. I knew then and there with the psychic experience that my feelings and invisible imagination were an absolute reality moving from the nonphysical world into the physical world toward me.

Visualization and imagination are only BUT Blasters when we use them in formats. Feeling good, feeling great, or having Energetic Multiple Orgasmic Combustion Points are pure vibrations magnetizing more good and more greatness to us. All too often, people choose to imagine or visualize the worst-case scenario. In fact, entire libraries have been written on the dark side of life in every category imaginable. I am not suggesting these books and other materials have no merit; I am saying that we can really use more material empowering each other to share in the soul kiss of our pure desires and heartfelt aspirations, to shine a light on the positive aspects in life and to simply talk about what we do love and appreciate in our now perspectives.

Last year, while working on the cable television program *Perspectives,* created by Marissa Kelley, Marissa and I had long conversations about the essence of the show and its purpose. We filmed *Perspectives* for over a year, during which time I secretly pretended and imagined with focused feelings that we were filming a show for network television. Marissa, our host Ellen Dostal, David Tillman, and I went through wardrobe, makeup, hair, set list, and program lineups. With each step forward, I practiced visualization and imagination techniques. I appreciated everyone on the set–both in front of and behind the cameras–who worked hard to make the show a success.

Roughly six months into filming, representatives from the FOX Network contacted me about doing a show they were putting together. To make a long story short, I met with executive producers, creators, and the head of FOX Television in Los Angeles to discuss filming a test pilot. Weeks later, a film crew was assembled and together we filmed all types of shoots for nearly 12 hours.

My focused imagination about a house for Mom came back to me in a psychic's prediction mere moments after I wrote of it. The energy I was putting out to the Universe with the show *Perspectives* came back to me six months later in the form of the FOX Network calling. And what began as a small, two-page class outline about Big BUTS has now manifested into this book.

George Bernard Shaw said, "Life isn't about finding yourself. Life is about creating yourself." Every day, I consciously choose to focus my imagination and visualization abilities into the areas of life that uplift, nurture, and serve me. I count blessings and look on the lighter side of life. I do this because it feels good to feel good. It feels good to have more solutions than problems and more positive things than negative things. It feels normal to focus on the light that I/we are than to focus my dominant attention into the dark. I believe we can uplift more people by standing and living in the light of our Soul Electricity.

Charles Lindbergh said, "It is the greatest shot of adrenaline to be doing what you've wanted to do so badly. You almost feel like you could fly without the plane." Appreciate your imagination and fly without the plane. Create positive realities in your imagination. Visualize a series of destinies that fit your wildest heaven-sent dreams. Write them, draw them, speak them, and share them with other people of like mind who support and appreciate your newfound desire to live the life you were born to enjoy.

BUT Blaster Ten   Day Dreams and Night Dreams

"If you will practice being fictional for awhile, you will understand that fictional characters are sometimes more real than people with bodies and heartbeats."

– *Richard Bach*

Before writing this book, I was diligently working on a novel based on historical events in the mid 1800s. The book, *A Walk Between Worlds,* weaves a fiction and nonfiction tapestry together as one. For years, I heard authors say their fictional characters came to life in their dreams and daydreams, acting out their parts for the author to record. In other words, the writer had put such pure emotional focus on his or her characters that the fictional characters themselves took on lives of their own.

The first time I heard comments like these, I thought to myself, "That is ridiculous!" Later, I realized firsthand how true their comments were.

At the gym, on a treadmill, with my stereo headset blaring in my ears is one of my favorite avenues to connect and communicate with the fictional characters in *A Walk Between Worlds*. I pick music that fits the essence of the scene that comes to me in my daydreams and imagination. While on the treadmill, I hold on tightly to the machine, close my eyes, and allow the dream world to come to me easily. I often keep pad and pen with me in order to capture the story on paper before I forget the information.

One day, there were only three people in the gym: Gene, the owner; another client; and me. I was at another pivotal point in the story. On this day, I was listening to Patti La Belle's *Greatest Hits* CD as scenes from the novel drifted in and out of my light dream state. Suddenly, the scenes dramatically lifted off the pages of my imagination and melded into a more concrete version inside my mind's eye. I felt highly charged emotion pouring forth from my heart and solar plexus area. My body began to subtly vibrate internally. Right before my eyes, the image of a hundred characters chained together in a swamp astral projected back in order to capture an amazing overhead shot. In one moment, I was seeing and feeling my chapters unfold and in the next moment, I was seeing a famous director surrounded with dozens of high-powered lights, endless crew members, and hundreds of extras shooting the footage from my book and creating a movie. Looking closer, I even saw myself standing in the woods by the swamp with other crew members.

In the scene, my dream personality had a realization. My dream self knew the moment the sun began dropping behind the tree-lined everglades that the actors and extras in the swamp would be eaten up by mosquitoes. When the director yelled, "Cut!" in his megaphone, I expressed my concern about the mosquitoes to him. Acting quickly, he sent runners to get ointment before the mosquitoes descended on their buffet of actors and extras.

The next scene jumped to every one of us on the crew, including the director, quickly rubbing gobs of ointment on the actors and extras for two reasons. We didn't want them to get eaten alive, and the director wanted to get the early evening sunset shots.

Many of us were waist-deep in swamp water, rubbing the talent with ointment while preparing for the final couple of shots for the day. Some people complained about the ointment's smell and its greasy texture against their skin. We apologized, saying it was all we could find on short notice and reminded them it would keep the bugs off.

While quickly applying ointment to my last actor, someone reached around and grabbed my calf. Because I wasn't expecting it, I jumped, which caused me to open my eyes.

I was a little startled to be in Sherman Oaks in a gym and on a treadmill after experiencing such a vivid, imaginative journey. Instinctively, I turned my head to see who had touched my calf. Gene was standing beside my treadmill rubbing his two fingers together and smelling them with a look of confusion on his face. He turned to the client he was training and said, "No, it's not Eddie either."

Stunned, I asked Gene why he'd touched my leg. Gene replied that he and his client began to smell some type of an ointment fragrance. He said the strong smell came from out of nowhere, and they couldn't trace the source of it. After the two of them checked themselves for the strange scent, Gene decided to check me. He rubbed the back of my leg to see if I was the source of the ointment! After the fact, I realized the amazing power of our conscious dreams and imagination.

In 2002, I was in a gym in Southern California daydreaming with fictional characters I had created. The characters in my book, some fiction and some nonfiction, lived in the southeastern United States a century and a half earlier. Across a span of 150 years and some 2,000 miles, two men smelled the ointment my dream crew rubbed onto actors and extras in a movie that had not been made from a book I have yet to finish.

Any time we purely hold the essence of our dreams and imagination, the Universe knocks itself out to bring that feeling into physical manifestation. Nighttime dreams, in my opinion, are more powerful than our daydreams. Why? Because when we sleep we are in the land of pure energy. We have no distractions, and certainly no Big BUTS. When our physical bodies are sleeping, our conscious thinking mind tiptoes to the back burner so our subconscious and super conscious can come out and play with our Heaven self.

We've all had premonitions and otherworldly experiences in our nighttime dreams. We can float, soar, fly, and create miracles in our dreams. We can future forecast and seek unlimited guidance directly from God Universe.

Nighttime dreams are BUT Free zones. In our dream experiences, our soul personality only enhances our strengths and our life purpose direction, sprinkling this knowledge into our daily lives like spiritually inspired fairy dust.

While writing her first book, *How To Be Happy,* Cynthia Richmond kept picturing the *Oprah* audience as the perfect customer for her book and what it offered. During this time, Cynthia had a dream in which she was watching *Oprah* on TV. During the show, Oprah held up Cynthia's book, looked into the camera, and said *How To Be Happy,* on the next *Oprah*!"

Some time later, Cynthia was actually on *Oprah* discussing a related topic. She gave Oprah her book during a commercial break. Oprah held Cynthia's book up and said, "How To Be Happy."

Even though the show Cynthia was on did not feature her new book, Cynthia can see and feel that her visualization + her imagination = a manifestation that reflected more of what is to come in her not-so-distant future. Cynthia's latest book, *Dream Power: Use Your Dreams to Change Your Life,* has given her national exposure as the country's leading dream expert. She has appeared on shows like *Oprah, The View, Politically Incorrect,* and *Leeza,* to name a few.

Cynthia is a beaming example of how we can use our daydreams and nighttime dreams as catalysts to create positive change in our daily lives. I have learned, sometimes the hard way, that if we do not consciously give our brain something to focus on, it will habitually repeat our old habits back to us over and over again.

If our old habits are low frequency, we will continue to create low-frequency circumstances. It is important to put our best dream foot forward in order to create the life that we have dreamt of living. Heck, what do we have to lose? Being happy?

12

The BUT Blaster Workout

Over the years, enthusiastic people have emailed and phoned a few of their favorite BUT Blasters. These are areas in their lives that lift them up from low-frequency funks to hi-frequency results. Over time, their habits of worry and fret began to melt away as they made a conscious decision to pick thoughts and feelings that radiate in their **Solar Plexus Megaphone**®.

This is a list of contributions "straight from the horse's mouth" that will assist you in raising emotions into the pure essence of your **Soul's Electricity**®.

I recommend you pick at least three points of focus each day. Do your first subject in the morning, the second in the middle of your day, and your last subject in the evening.

This list is designed to assist you in focusing on subjects that amplify good, positive emotions. Whenever possible, lock your Focused Feelings onto the subject that resonates with your desire to raise your vibration for 30 seconds to two minutes at a time. Hold the subject in your mind and in your Solar Plexus Megaphone®. Feel the animated essence of the subject you have chosen.

This "feel good" discipline can assist in eliminating your Big BUT and over time can amplify and build you to more thought and feelings which, in turn, will promote and magnetize your dreams. Let the BUT Blaster Games begin.

People Laughing	Natural Beauty	Expressing Humor
Newborn Babies	Smiles	Puppies or Kittens
Sincere People	Acts of Kindness	Happiness
Wellbeing	Joy	Win-Win Situations
Positive Outcomes	Pure Desire	A Soft Breeze
Crisp Morning Air	Radiant Dreaming	Music
Song	Dance	Favorite Quotes
Reading	Passion	Inspiration
Accomplishment	Standing Ovation	Meditation
Creativity	Appreciation	Déjà Vu
Clear Intention	Knowledge	Freedom
Sunlight	Moonlight	Starlight
Great Friendships	Cartoons	Sitcoms
Hilarious Jokes	Confidence	Self Love
Spirituality	Soul Focus	Feeling Supported
Divination	Allowing Good	Feeling Good
Abundance	Prosperity	Radiating God Self
Sincerity	Life Purpose	Ease
Synchronicity	Goose Bumps	Loving Memories
Intuition	Feeling Great	Decadent Food
Travel	Healing Journeys	Visualization
Reiki	Massage	Hot Showers
Rituals	Miracles	Counting Blessings
Chanting	Enlightenment	Afternoon Naps
Honesty	Feeling Special	Self Appreciation

Do you have a BUT Blaster suggestion to add to the list? If so, this is the perfect place to add them.

13

The Feel Good Life

Today, in this moment, make a conscious hi-frequency decision to move through your life knowing you are in the OVAL Mirror of life. This mirror is unconditional love, and it only says yes to your vibration 24/7. It supports your dreams, goals, and aspirations. It brings you solutions and clarity. And, at the exact same time, the OVAL Mirror supports your negative emotions, low-frequency thoughts, and self-inflicted shortcomings, which, in turn, bring you more problems and obscurity.

Whatever "invisible" feelings you choose to radiate are reflected in the "invisible" OVAL Mirror, and the OVAL Mirror then manifests your feelings back to you physically. Do things, Think things, and Feel things inside that activate Good Feelings. This is a beautiful form of self-love that will enhance your life tenfold.

Create a prosperity commitment. Every moment you think of it, do a Feel Good Free-For-All ritual. Observe everything you can that makes you feel good. If there is not a pleasant physical environment around you that feels good, create the ideal environment in your imagination. Do this with the power of your Intuitive Intellect and beef it up with a ramped-up Energetic Multiple Orgasmic Combustion Point.

14

Your Soul Affirming Oath

It is hard to believe we have come to the end of our journey together. Though this is the completion of the mental material, I also feel it marks a new beginning. I think of this material as a pristine lake of crystal-clear consciousness; each new belief generated in your mind as a result of these pages is equivalent to dropping pebbles of pure intention into your new perspective, thus creating a new beginning using hi-frequency tools designed to enhance the quality of your life.

I thank you with all my heart and soul for taking this spiritual adventure with me. I am appreciative and grateful for our time together.

I want to close the book with an oath of intention. I suggest that you playfully recite this oath each morning as you wake before starting your day, and again each night before falling asleep. Remember the power and vibration of using your Intuitive Intellect as you speak or think each word. Allow the feeling frequency of each word to resonate and vibrate purely inside of each and every atom, molecule and cell.

Why?

Because each night as we sleep, we merge into our soul consciousness and become the pure essence of the Universe, and each morning as we awaken, we are strongly connected to our universeal power. The longer we are physically awake, the more we accidentally get distracted by mundane, insignificant things that do not serve our higher good.

Reciting this oath with the frequency of your intuitive soul and your human intellect can create a masterful bridge of light over the pristine lake of consciousness. Think of each pebble of pure intention that you drop into the lake as aligning you with your much deserved life. As a result, you are leaving your BIG BUT behind and enhancing your love, money, and career.

Practice saying this light-hearted mantra for the next 30 to 45 day cycle or until you become consciously aware that you are observing pleasant things that make you feel good. Before you realize it, you will have developed a soulful habit of observing hi-frequency persons, places, and things in your physical world and in your mental thoughts and imagination.

Happy creating and blessings to you always!

At last, your Soul Affirming Oath:

Today, I will consciously stand in the OVAL Mirror of life, applying the TAGS Technique in brilliant harmony with my higher self.

If I accidentally commit a Big BUT travesty, I will gladly employ the 1-2-3s of the B-U-T, Big BUT Stand-ins, or my AND Avalanches.

As a Soul Artist creating my life, I will choose to feel good, laugh hard, and laugh often. I will get out in nature and listen to music that inspires and uplifts my Earth Self and my Heaven Self as ONE.

I will pray with a pure heart while using Vibratory Vocabulary that activates my Soul Electricity.

I will day dream, visualize, and imagine the best-case scenarios possible, and I will do all of this while wearing my Thinking C.A.P.

I promise to happily celebrate and appreciate people, lovely places, flawless circumstances, and happy situations at least a dozen times a day until I graduate to doing this at least a hundred times a week.

I will start NOW! And so it is!

A Sincere Thank You

I hope you had as much fun reading, *A Southern Psychic's Guide to Fixin' the Big BUT Syndrome,* as I did repackaging it.

As a small gift of appreciation for your purchase of this book I've added two chapters from my upcoming book, *"Memoirs of A Southern Psychic – Ghosts, Angels, and Other Deep-Fried Miracles.*

I hope you enjoy it. Thank you again.

Until we meet again, be sure to keep your thoughts, feelings, and frequencies high, fast, and pure so that you can unlock the Universe within.

Eddie

Eddie

About the Author

Eddie Conner is a Radio Host, Author, Humorist, Soul Intuitive, Keynote Speaker, and the Creator of Meta-Fun-ics, *Making Metaphysics Fun.*

Eddie has appeared on *America's Best TV Show*, Australia's, *The Morning Show, John Edward's InfiniteQuest.com, CNN.com, Instinct Magazine, Associated Press, Coast-to-Coast with George Noory,* and featured in *CBSLocal.com* for their, *Best Psychics and Mediums in Los Angeles* issue.

Eddie's Soul Intuitive abilities naturally led him to hosting shows for *CRN Radio, KIEV AM-FM, LA Talk Radio, Global Voice Broadcasting Radio, and UBN Radio* where he co-hosts, *Truth Be Told with Tony & Eddie,* doing celebrity interviews and also hosting, *Girl Your Soul is Speaking, Unlock the Universe Within,* and *Sound Bites for the Soul* segments.

An accomplished seminar leader and co-founder of, *Sail into Your Soul — A Journey into Bliss*, Eddie leads world tours and spiritual travel adventures to the Far East, The Mexican Rivera, Alaska, Hawaii, Machu Picchu, Peru, Ireland, Aruba, Patagonia, and The Galápagos Islands.

Eddie is amazing at elevating television, radio, and seminar audiences higher into the rich world of his BUT-Free Living principles, trademarked language, and leading edge methodologies.

Visit Eddie at EddieConner.com

Eddie Conner / Soul Awareness
3940 Laurel Canyon Blvd. #138
Studio City, California   91604

Memoirs of A Southern Psychic
Ghosts, Angels, and Other Deep-Fried Miracles

Prologue

High Point, North Carolina   1981

The afternoon a speeding car slammed into my borrowed station wagon, crashing it into a utility pole, I had recently graduated high school, was in a bad relationship, working two jobs, and babysitting to earn gas money.

Just before impact, the world around me entered a state of slow motion, like in a dream. I was pulled high above my body and into a surreal consciousness.

From overhead I watched another car T-bone mine, crushing both cars into a pile of screeching, mangled wreckage. Moving further skyward I noticed my busted windows splintering across the streets, reflecting tiny diamonds of light within the shards. It was at that moment, when the glass sparkles detonated that I realized I no longer felt a connection to my body. Every sound and earthly feeling disappeared far below while I was swept further upward.

It's true what people say about near death experiences – your life flashes before your eyes and the light wraps you inside its refuge, away from pain. I floated there while buried memories of my early life blazed before me in an odd series of rapid flashbacks:

- Me playing with my twin sister who no one else could see.

- Dad beating my pregnant Momma in front of me.

- Grandma doing an exorcism to clear me of demons she claimed had possessed me.

- Dad yelling, shaking me at his eye level before launching me against a wall.

- The ghost on Grandma's porch who disappeared into thin air seconds before I touched him.

- The first time I saw angels.

This final memory gave way to every psychic recollection and angelic visitation I'd ever had, until each experience funneled into a reflective reservoir within me.

As I watched my child self talking to my angels, I heard in the distance below me ambulance sirens and police radios. I felt chaos boiling around me, and my astral body grew dim. I remember thinking that I didn't want the light to leave me behind as it had many times before. Suddenly I was dropped from blissful perfection and back into a battered, leaden body.

I gasped, "The kids! The kids!"

As paramedics loaded me into an ambulance a fireman said, "There were not any kids in the car."

Thank God, because I had specifically borrowed the station wagon to pick up the four little munchkins I was babysitting that afternoon. I had it in my mind they were with me. Thankfully they were not.

I was released from the emergency room that night, then, against my better judgment, ended up with my lover, Lee, at Godfather's Pizza on North Main. My head, neck and back were in severe pain but I had to pretend to feel okay, because Lee wanted to do something besides sit at home and watch me recuperate. While waiting for our pizza, Lee kept feeding quarters into the Pac Man machine and drinking draft beer. I went to the men's room to decompress. Once alone in the stall, I realized it was the first time I'd been by myself in weeks, and it was a relief. I was able to quiet my mind and recall my earlier experience.

My first significant observation was that while I was in the light, I hadn't experienced myself as the insecure kid everyone had bullied and made fun of. I wasn't a victim of poverty and negative self-image, nor did I feel the typical desire to try and fit in with the crowds that had made my adolescent life a living hell.

Then it hit me; over the years I had purposely suppressed my sensitive, artistic and intuitive skills, and was taught to believe these qualities made me weak and sissified. I'd withdrawn and buried my gifts.

In the light I wasn't broken. From its expansive perspective I recognized that my childhood desires and questions were not in vain, then understood my hardships were essentially thousands of blessings.

"But, what's my purpose?" I thought.

A commode flushed in an adjoining stall.

"Wow, I hope that's not a sign."

The contrast between how I perceived myself in the light versus how I felt in everyday life was staggering. Had I unconsciously thought of myself as a victim of circumstances? Had my belief of having no self worth finally led to withering in despair over the years? The thought made me shiver.

As a child, I'd seen the light before, because that was how my angels always entered my room. Having freshly reemerged from this illuminated environment hours earlier, I had the distinct understanding that the person I was in the light was also the person I had the potential to be every day – if I chose it.

Something else peculiar happened during my time out-of-body. I had felt compassion and love for my dad, step-father, and my grandma during my flashbacks. While suspended above the wreck I didn't judge or blame them, but once I reentered my body the hurt and anger I'd harbored for them clouded my thoughts once again.

In essence, I learned happiness is ours for the taking, but we have to do something to create it for ourselves. I certainly wasn't happy. I'd stayed in a miserable relationship far too long with Lee, constantly forgetting that it takes two healthy people to make a couple work.

I enjoyed my co-workers, but hated my dead-end jobs, which didn't inspire intuition or creativity. The fact was, I'd been fed up for a couple of years, settling for the minimum wage paychecks that the world of textile mills, babysitting, and fast food had meagerly provided.

Because of the car accident I was able to revisit my true essence; a miraculous experience. As a result, I made a deliberate choice to be happy and do what I loved. This thought made me feel light again. I smiled, excited to start utilizing my strengths. I'd always wanted to uplift others in a fun, intuitive way, and after the day I'd had, I figured today was the perfect day to start.

I felt Lee's impatience pulling my attention back to the restaurant. I flushed the toilet, and washed my hands. Then, inside the men's restroom, I made a silent vow that come hell or high water, I'd figure out what my true purpose was and be happy doing what I loved, even if it killed me.

That night I barely slept. Images of the accident replayed in my mind. Each time I almost fell asleep another memory broke through as though I was swimming in calm, warm waters filled with intuitive treasures from my childhood.

Finally, I got up, grabbed my pen and journal. I decided that if I was going to gain clarity on what had happened I'd have to go back 20 years to understand my angels, the light, and other out-of-body experiences I'd had growing up.

I leaned back in my chair, careful not to strain my neck and back. "Wow," I thought, "I can't believe I remembered my angels."

I wrote, "High Point, N.C." and "1963-64" in my journal, then closed my eyes. Being a simple southern boy, I wanted to go back to the very beginning and lasso every single ghost, angel, and deep-fried miracle.

Memoirs of A Southern Psychic
Ghosts, Angels & Other Deep-Fried Miracles
Chapter 1

High Point, North Carolina   1963 - 64

Grandma was a strong, spirited lumberjack of a woman with a booming voice and wicked backhand that could sting your face for hours. After braiding her long, gray hair, she knotted it up in a scarf around her head that matched her imitation pearl cat-eyeglasses. Her clothes were fabric scraps she hand-sewed into a hodgepodge of garments that loosely covered her ample frame. Other accessories included yard shoes with toe holes, her butterbean gardening hat, and a set of chipped dentures her dog had gotten ahold of, leaving them riddled with canine teeth marks and one less tooth for Grandma.

Grandma rented an old, rundown property off Highway 62, surrounded by oak trees and thousands of flowers, plants, and creeping ivy vines. Over time, her house reminded me of the old witch's place in the Hansel and Gretel story, minus the cookies and candy. The first thing you felt when approaching were thick waves of suffocating heat smacking the life from your body.

Walking through her front door, your breath and sight were pinched off by unseen forces. Her two wood-burning stoves stole your breath first, followed by temporary blindness brought on by soot-covered walls, grimy pictures and second-hand furniture. Once your eyes adjusted to the dark, closed-in space, dozens of filmy pictures of Jesus watched your every move.

Everywhere you looked, there was Jesus on a cross, Jesus wearing a crown of thorns, or bloody Jesus expressing agony. There was only one serene Jesus image imprisoned inside a tarnished, ornate gold frame with a built-in tube light that accentuated his face. Any remaining wall space was peppered with decorative crosses, photos of her grandkids, lacquered biblical quotes, and angelic pictures.

Once inside, the sounds of traffic zipping along the highway mixed with firewood popping in the stove's steel stomach, as food boiled, fried, simmered or baked. From her bedroom blared a preacher's words struggling past the static of a choppy AM radio signal. The sermon was often followed by an elderly white gospel choir whose droning sounded more like dying cows in a hailstorm than the intended heavenly message.

"Children are to be seen, not heard," Grandma preached. "Don't speak unless you're spoken to." I had learned the hard way that her rules changed faster than Dad's moods, and going against her orders often meant a severe beating, or worse.

On this particular visit I was two years old and Bobby was an infant, when Momma took us to visit Grandma. Bobby slept between propped up pillows in the living room while Momma and I sat in Grandma's hot, muggy kitchen.

The small kitchen was stuffed with a faded refrigerator, huge deep-freezer, wood stove, and a homemade countertop, with plastic tubs for washing dishes with well water. The table and chairs were pushed flush against stained walls, and every surface was covered with heaps of canned goods, old bakery products, paper bags, pie tins and cooking utensils.

Momma fanned her blouse to generate cool air, when Grandma gave me a block of wood to play with. For some reason I threw it on the floor. Infuriated, Grandma popped me hard, then sharply jammed the block back into my hands. Crying, I dropped it, and with my arms held high I reached for Momma to hold me.

Grandma took ahold of my shirt, spun me around, and spanked my rear end. While hitting me she looked Momma square in the face and said, "Now you whip him too."

Instinctively, Momma pulled me back into her arms. Assuming Momma had misunderstood her, Grandma repeated, "I told you to whip him; not fuss over him!"

Teetering on the double-edged sword of being Grandma's middle daughter of thirteen children, and a teenage mother to me, Momma tried to sound respectful while standing her ground.

"No ma'am, I'm not going to hit him."

Grandma wiped sweat from her brow with the back of her hand then dried it on her apron. "What?" she shrieked, while retrieving the wooden block again.

Momma watched her in vain. "He doesn't understand why you're whipping him."

Ignoring Momma's protest, Grandma jabbed the block at me a third time. Balling my hands beneath my chin I plastered my body against Momma so Grandma couldn't reach my hind-end. Aggravated, she chunked the wood behind the stove and then spanked my bare legs harder. I cried louder. Momma stood up, grabbed Grandma's blistering hands, and when that didn't work, Momma pushed her away from me.

"Stop it," Momma said clenching her jaw, her body shielding me as Grandma swatted around Momma's hands to reach me. "I said, STOP IT!"

Grandma took a step back, and sent her daughter through seven circles of hell with her gaze. "What did you say to me?"

Pulling sweat soaked hair off her neck and flipping it over her shoulders Momma stood up, out of breath. "He didn't do anything wrong."

Grandma advanced, her voice matching the stove's overpowering heat. "You don't understand do you? You've got to break his spirit now or he'll run you for the rest of your life!"

Her words stunned Momma. Neither of them spoke for the longest time. Finally, Grandma turned her back to us, pretending to wash dishes in water she'd been boiling on the stove.

Momma gathered up our things, wrapped Bobby in a blanket, and walked us back into the cramped kitchen to say goodbye and thank Grandma for the fatback biscuits and sweet tea. We walked through the Jesus gallery to the porch. I quietly closed the screen door while Momma situated, Bobby, his things, and her pocketbook.

That's when I saw a thin, wispy image of a man's face, suspended in midair, watching us.

I closed my eyes then rubbed them open, but the man's face had already vanished. Momma took my hand again. I glanced back over my shoulder as we left the porch, in case the man's face was still there. But he was gone.

I was confused about why Grandma had whipped me. After that day I grew more afraid of her ever-changing moods, which put her in the same no-win category as my Daddy.

Playing back the incident, I knew it had taken all Momma's nerve to stand up to Grandma, but my young mind still couldn't make sense of grown-ups. As we walked to the bus stop that afternoon, Momma's hand had eventually stopped shaking and I remember glancing up to see her face, trying to imagine what she might be thinking. Though she looked straight ahead, her face unreadable to the outside world, I knew she was hurting inside but she never mentioned the incident with Grandma again. Neither did I.

I hungered to understand why bad things happened to people I loved, and why people I loved treated each other so badly. I knew Daddy loved Momma, but back then I couldn't make sense out of him beating her or us. And then there was Grandma's unpredictable craziness, all in the name of God. When she got on a roll, it seemed everyone feared her and nobody escaped her temper.

Every night I'd secretly pray and ask for help to understand what made people happy, what made them sad, and how I might help them. I figured that once I got acceptable answers, I might understand how to turn a lot of these bad family experiences into something shiny and new again, especially for Momma.

After we got home, I thought about the eerie, cloudy face that had been watching us on Grandma's porch. Misty and vapor-like, he had floated from nowhere before disappearing into thin air. I'd never seen anything like it. It made me feel strange and uncomfortable, like I wasn't allowed to be there. I wondered if the wispy face would return.

www.ingramcontent.com/pod-product-compliance
Lightning Source LLC
Chambersburg PA
CBHW020615300426
44113CB00007B/653